The Living Image

Rich —

So much you have been to me and done for me. Thank you!

I love you as a father, a dear friend, a brother and a mentor. The Lord bless and keep you! With you for His Glory.

Tony

The Living Image

GOD PURPOSED YOU TO BEAR HIS IMAGE AND KNOW HIS WILL

A.M. LAMOURIA

TATE PUBLISHING & Enterprises

Published by Tate Publishing & Enterprises, LLC
127 E. Trade Center Terrace | Mustang, Oklahoma 73064 USA
1.888.361.9473 | www.tatepublishing.com

Tate Publishing is committed to excellence in the publishing industry. The company reflects the philosophy established by the founders, based on Psalm 68:11,
"The Lord gave the word and great was the company of those who published it."

Book design copyright © 2009 by Tate Publishing, LLC. All rights reserved.
Interior design by Joey Garrett

Published in the United States of America

ISBN: 978-1-60696-547-4
1. Religion / Christian Life / Spiritual Growth
2. Religion / Christian Ministry / Discipleship
09.03.26

To my Heavenly Father, for His glory.
To Eli, Zac, and Luc, may you know the Creator and
Savior of your souls. May He cause His face to shine
upon you, and may yours shine for Him willingly.

Acknowledgments

- Elisabeth, for your patience and love through slow days and long nights, waiting.

- Mom, for always believing in me.

- Harold and Carol, for always, always being there and here and everywhere in between.

- My professors at Grand Rapids Theological Seminary and Northwest Baptist Seminary who took the time to mentor me and critique my thoughts.

- Pastor Doug Crawford, Pastor Mark Cizauskas, and Pastor John Nixon, for your oversight, patience, and encouragement.

- Gene Rogers, for being a mentor, a friend, and a trusted proofreader.

- Lisa Miller, for putting in the many hours of editing and fielding questions about pretty much anything.

- The youth and family at Sylvan Way Baptist Church, for encouraging, believing, and sharing with me.

Table of Contents

Introduction:

What is Life All About?

As I look back on twenty years of knowing Christ, I appreciate the struggles that have led me to where I am today. However, my heart also grieves when I think about the shame my pride produced in that time and the ignorance that my stubbornness brought to light. I was one of those young Christians who thought I knew it all and had all the knowledge I needed in order to make clear decisions when life presented complex problems. But I never have known it all, and I thank God for those who had patience enough to let me run around with blindfolds on until I was ready to accept that I needed help in taking them off.

In my life, I have been blessed with incredible, godly teachers. My professors, friends, pastors, parents, and my wife have all contributed to my understanding of what God's Word reveals. However, it was in the aftermath of an explosion in Iraq and reflection on a few good books when all of these influences converged into an understanding of what it really means to live in His will and to be an Image Bearer, no matter what I do with my life.

I spent many years of my Christian life frustrated and

fatigued by the disciplines of trying to be holy and following what I perceived as God's will for my life without assurance that I actually was living out His will for me. It was a continual struggle to believe in myself as an Image Bearer when I was constantly confronted with the depravity within myself. I constantly worried that I had ruined any intended goodness God had planned for me because of poor choices and sin. I struggled to hear or see God reveal His will to me in order for me to take the next step. As I later learned, the struggle was not due to God's ambiguity but my own undisciplined wanderings.

I graduated from a Christian university with a degree in youth ministry and adolescent development. After a brief stint working for a church and returning to graduate school, I joined the Marine Corps for five years and subsequently entered seminary in Grand Rapids, Michigan. In 2006 I took a pause in my seminary training to return to the Marine Corps and serve a tour in Iraq as an infantry officer. I had been off active duty for nearly two years, and to go back in after several semesters in seminary, for me, was a drastic change in perspective as to what it meant to serve God and serve man in such a unique situation. This was the beginning of a life-changing process for me.

While in seminary, I read several books that had a tremendous impact on my spiritual development. I took these books with me and pored over them while working through my deployment. As I did, I began to understand that my perceptions of what it meant *to bear the Image of God* and *to know His will* were both significantly misguided. This book is taken from that journey and the lessons I learned from it.

I wish that somebody had given me a book like this

when I was younger. I wish I had been able to grasp some of the truths in this book before I had headed off to college. It probably would have grounded my very idealistic and passionate heart and saved me from some of the pain caused by my own immature faith. There is nothing wrong with a passionate faith, mind you; however, it would have been nice to have had that passion tempered with a mature understanding of my responsibility as an Image Bearer in creation and the joyful freedom of being human.

This book is an introduction to a much deeper spiritual journey that each individual must take on his or her own. There is nothing new in this book; it is simply an encouragement to take another look at the story of Genesis through Revelation in order to prompt the reader to explore certain issues sooner rather than later.

First, I wanted to remind the next generation that God's story is a perfect and sufficient testimony of God's sovereignty, revealed purposes, and instruction for life and salvation. It is becoming more and more apparent in today's culture that the essential truths of the Christian gospel and faith are under attack even from within the Church itself. Modern and postmodern thought are both challenging the foundational truths of Christ's claims: 1) that Christ is the only way unto salvation, 2) that the Body of Christ is made up of only those who confess this truth, and 3) that Scripture is absolute truth and authority.

Second, I wrote this book to remind everyone that the purpose for every human life is found early in Scripture and that it is not a mystery. God uniquely designed each one of us for a purpose. Our purpose is to glorify God by bearing His Image. If that purpose is learned early in life rather than later, I believe it will lead people to read Scripture through the lens of the theological worldview with which God intended for us to approach Scripture. I believe it would also lead to fulfillment in life and repentance from ungodly pursuits that we often use to try to replace our original purpose.

God commanded his chosen people early in His great story to tell the future generations of His wonders and revelations, lest they forget about all that He has done and who He is. There are a few notably strong voices within the evangelical Christian community today who are striving to remind the Church of God's unchanging truth and His eternal purposes. However, with such a cacophony of religious garbage mixed in with the truth, today's students are evermore willing to listen to the "popular" over the fundamental. I hope this book is a guide back to Scripture and the Church that lives it out responsibly.

One last thing—and this is paramount—I believe in the absolute authority of Scripture. I believe there are answers in the Bible meant for us to know and that we can, in fact, know them. Furthermore, I believe that the Bible was intended to be a source of wisdom for the believer and that every believer is not only able to know but commanded by the Bible itself to know the wisdom and answers it has to provide for the proper stewardship of this life as it pertains to knowing God's will and bearing His Image.

I challenge you to humble your spirit and quiet your mind as you read through this book. I also point you toward the works cited in this writing as invaluable resources of mature insight and products of faithful stewardship in the area of biblical hermeneutics. This is a purposefully systematic approach to two simple, yet deeply profound, theological truths: We were created in His Image, and we were purposed to know His will.

If you are ready, and if you long to see your purpose in life at work, or if you are simply about to set out on some new adventure in life, then I invite you to look again at what it means to be an Image Bearer living out the will of God in your life.

Worldview: Why It Matters

Without having a clear understanding of what a worldview really is and what *your* individual worldview actually is, you will have a difficult time fitting your spiritual training into a cohesive grid of understanding that establishes spiritual maturity. In other words, without a worldview in which to translate your experiences and your knowledge, you simply gain more experience and facts. But with the proper worldview to translate your experience, you don't just absorb—you grow, learn, and most importantly, change to reflect Christ!

Without a foundational worldview through which all spiritual training can be sifted and tested, faith ends up being free spirited and at the whim of whatever personality most affects it.

Let me use an example from sports. For now I'll start with wrestling (real wrestling). In wrestling, if an individual possesses a natural ability to grapple, he may do well and go a long time as a fair competitor. But raw skill can only take one so far. If the basic aptitude to grapple is not honed with intelligent training in flexibility, fluidity, offensive and defensive techniques, specific moves, the ability to move without forecasting your movements, the ability to see your opponent's moves before he or she makes them, and the ability to think faster and move faster than your opponent in a controlled manner, then you may end up hurting yourself and your opponent. Without a proper perspective and respect for the competition itself, then even the naturally gifted athlete can appear to be reckless and immature. With the proper perspective and respect, he or she changes into a formidable opponent *because of the knowledge he or she uses to apply his or her skill.*

Faith, likewise, demands a proper perspective and respect before it can mature. Without a foundational worldview through which all spiritual training can be sifted and tested, faith ends up being free spirited and at the whim of whatever personality most affects it. Paul warns Timothy of this exact thing in 2 Timothy, chapters 3–4.

> But realize this, that in the last days difficult times will come. For men will be lovers of self, lovers of money, boastful, arrogant, revilers, disobedient to parents, ungrateful, unholy, unloving, irreconcilable, malicious gossips, without self-control, brutal, haters of good, treacherous, reckless, conceited, lovers of pleasure rather than lovers of God, holding to a form of godliness, although they have denied its power; Avoid such men as these. For among them are those who enter into households and

captivate weak women weighed down with sins, led on by various impulses, always learning and never able to come to the knowledge of the truth. Just as Jannes and Jambres opposed Moses, so these men also oppose the truth, men of depraved mind, rejected in regard to the faith. But they will not make further progress; for their folly will be obvious to all, just as Jannes's and Jambres's folly was also.

Now you followed my teaching, conduct, purpose, faith, patience, love, perseverance, persecutions, and sufferings, such as happened to me at Antioch, at Iconium and at Lystra; what persecutions I endured, and out of them all the Lord rescued me! Indeed, all who desire to live godly in Christ Jesus will be persecuted. But evil men and impostors will proceed from bad to worse, deceiving and being deceived. You, however, continue in the things you have learned and become convinced of, knowing from whom you have learned them, and that from childhood you have known the sacred writings which are able to give you the wisdom that leads to salvation through faith which is in Christ Jesus.

All Scripture is inspired by God and profitable for teaching, for reproof, for correction, for training in righteousness; so that the man of God may be adequate, equipped for every good work.

I solemnly charge you in the presence of God and of Christ Jesus, who is to judge the living and the dead, and by His appearing and His kingdom: preach the word; be ready in season and out of season; reprove, rebuke, exhort, with great patience and instruction. For the time will come when they will not endure sound doctrine; but wanting to have their ears tickled, they will accumulate for themselves teachers in accordance to their own desires, and will turn away their ears from the truth and will turn aside to myths. But you, be sober in all things, endure hardship, do the work of an evangelist, fulfill your ministry.

2 Timothy 3:1–4:5

There are some modern examples of this. The current discussions surrounding the emergent church and postmodernism are a good example of this. If the worldview of individuals involved in directing a local body of believers is that the Church was instituted by Christ for the purpose of evangelizing the lost and making the local church comfortable and appealing to the masses, then the local church will look dramatically different than those churches which hold to the worldview that the Body, as Christ instituted it, is for believers to come together for worship, instruction, fellowship, and growth. We will talk more later about why evangelism is a mandate of the Church, not the purpose for it.

A good example of someone with a biblical worldview would be Martin Luther, who, upon understanding grace as it was related in Romans, was able to develop a new worldview of God and man that allowed for the development of biblical systematic theology as we know it today. His worldview changed the lives of millions, if not billions, of people throughout history by giving them a proper framework through which to translate God's grace through the biblical narrative.

Your life may not revolve around such drastic issues from day to day, but the principle is the same. We all begin with something very small. That thing is an idea. Maybe your initial idea comes from the Bible. Maybe it comes from a pastor. Maybe it comes from friends or parents or just personal experience. Wherever it comes from, that idea about what life is all about is the seed that will grow into and develop a worldview. So the first question is where does your worldview come from? Where should it come from?

The Biblical Genesis

The book of Genesis appears at the beginning of the Bible for this reason. It *is* the beginning. Genesis is God's direction for establishing a proper worldview. It's important to note that God's first worldview was not scientific; it was theological (at least, that's what we call it today). It's not so important whether or not the six-day creation is literal or figurative. God didn't intend for it to be a provable scientific fact (otherwise it would be); rather, he intended for it to establish a worldview!

Take a look at the story. Take note that the main thrust of the story is God at work, not the work itself.

> In the beginning God created the heavens and the earth. The earth was formless and void, and darkness was over the surface of the deep, and the Spirit of God was moving over the surface of the waters. Then God said, "Let there be light"; and there was light.

God saw that the light was good; and God separated the light from the darkness.

God called the light day, and the darkness He called night And there was evening and there was morning, one day.

Then God said, "Let there be an expanse in the midst of the waters, and let it separate the waters from the waters." God made the expanse, and separated the waters which were below the expanse from the waters which were above the expanse; and it was so.

God called the expanse heaven. And there was evening and there was morning, a second day.

Then God said, "Let the waters below the heavens be gathered into one place, and let the dry land appear"; and it was so. God called the dry land earth, and the gathering of the waters He called seas; and God saw that it was good.

Then God said, "Let the earth sprout vegetation, plants yielding seed, and fruit trees on the earth bearing fruit after their kind with seed in them"; and it was so. The earth brought forth vegetation, plants yielding seed after their kind, and trees bearing fruit with seed in them, after their kind; and God saw that it was good. There was evening and there was morning, a third day.

Then God said, "Let there be lights in the expanse of the heavens to separate the day from the night, and let them be for signs and for seasons and for days and years; and let them be for lights in the expanse of the heavens to give light on the earth"; and it was so.

God made the two great lights, the greater light to govern the day, and the lesser light to govern the night; He made the stars also. God placed them in the expanse of the heavens to give light on the earth, and to govern the day and the night, and to separate the light from the darkness; and God saw that it was good. There was evening and there was morning, a fourth day.

Then God said, "Let the waters teem with swarms of living creatures, and let birds fly above the earth in the open expanse of the heavens." God created the great sea monsters and every living creature that moves, with which the waters swarmed after their kind, and every winged bird after its kind; and God saw that it was good. God blessed them, saying, "Be fruitful and multiply, and fill the waters in the seas, and let birds multiply on the earth." There was evening and there was morning, a fifth day.

Then God said, "Let the earth bring forth living creatures after their kind: cattle and creeping things and beasts of the earth after their kind"; and it was so.

God made the beasts of the earth after their kind, and the cattle after their kind, and everything that creeps on the ground after its kind; and God saw that it was good.

Then God said, "Let Us make man in Our image, according to Our likeness; and let them rule over the fish of the sea and over the birds of the sky and over the cattle and over all the earth, and over every creeping thing that creeps on the earth."

God created man in His own image, in the image of God He created him; male and female He created them. God blessed them; and God said to them, "Be fruitful and multiply, and fill the earth, and subdue it; and rule over the fish of the sea and over the birds of the sky and over every living thing that moves on the earth."

Then God said, "Behold, I have given you every plant yielding seed that is on the surface of all the earth, and every tree which has fruit yielding seed; it shall be food for you;

and to every beast of the earth and to every bird of the sky and to every thing that moves on the earth which has life, I have given every green plant for food"; and it was so.

God saw all that He had made, and behold, it was very good. And there was evening and there was morning, the sixth day. Thus the heavens and the earth were completed, and all their hosts. By the seventh day God completed His work which He had done, and He rested on the seventh day from all His work which He had done. Then God blessed the seventh day and sanctified it, because in it He rested from all His work which God had created and made.

Genesis 1:1–2:3

It's not about the six days of creation. It's about the sovereignty and purpose of God. We learn nothing about science or history (except where we came from) from that narrative. But we do learn about God. So before we go any further, let's ask what God meant for us to get out of the first chapter of the Bible. It appears that he wanted us to think about everything that comes after the first chapter with a few things in mind.

God wanted us to know that He was, is, and always will be the supreme being who is always in control and is always the central figure. Everything that comes after chapter one of Genesis needs to be looked at through this worldview. That means that the only source for our worldview to develop from is Scripture. This is why Scripture declares over and over again, in subtle and not so subtle ways, that our life experience is not to be used to interpret Scripture, but we are to use Scripture to interpret life experiences. Look at these passages of Scripture:

> Therefore did that which is good become a cause of death for me? May it never be! Rather it was sin, in order that it might be shown to be sin by effecting my death through that which is good, so that through the commandment sin would become utterly sinful. For we know that the Law is spiritual, but I am of flesh, sold into bondage to sin. For what I am doing, I do not understand; for I am not practicing what I would like to do, but I am doing the very thing I hate. But if I do the very thing I do not want to do, I agree with the Law, confessing that the Law is good. So now, no longer am I the

one doing it, but sin which dwells in me. For I know that nothing good dwells in me, that is, in my flesh; for the willing is present in me, but the doing of the good is not. For the good that I want, I do not do, but I practice the very evil that I do not want. But if I am doing the very thing I do not want, I am no longer the one doing it, but sin which dwells in me.

I find then the principle that evil is present in me, the one who wants to do good. For I joyfully concur with the law of God in the inner man, but I see a different law in the members of my body, waging war against the law of my mind and making me a prisoner of the law of sin which is in my members. Wretched man that I am! Who will set me free from the body of this death? Thanks be to God through Jesus Christ our Lord! So then, on the one hand I myself with my mind am serving the law of God, but on the other, with my flesh the law of sin.

Romans 7:13–25

And do not be conformed to this world, but be transformed by the renewing of your mind, so that you may prove what the will of God is, that which is good and acceptable and perfect.

Romans 12:2

And my message and my preaching were not in persuasive words of wisdom, but in demonstration of the Spirit and of power, so that your faith would not rest on the wisdom of men, but on the power of God.

1 Corinthians 2: 4–5

Concerning him we have much to say, and it is hard to explain, since you have become dull of hearing. For though by this time you ought to be teachers, you have need again for someone to teach you the elementary principles of the oracles of God, and you have come to need milk and not solid food. For everyone who partakes only of milk is not accustomed to the word of righteousness, for he is an infant. But solid food is for the mature, who because of practice have their senses trained to discern good and evil.

Hebrews 5:11–14

… as also in all his letters, speaking in them of these things, in which are some things hard to understand, which the untaught and unstable distort, as they do also the rest of the Scriptures, to their own destruction. You therefore, beloved, knowing this beforehand, be on your guard so that you are not carried away by the error of unprincipled men and fall from your own steadfastness, but grow in the grace and knowledge of our Lord and Savior Jesus Christ To Him be the glory, both now and to the day of eternity. Amen.

2 Peter 3:16–18

Think about this. How many people in this world decide to translate scriptural truths in a way that supports what they have personally experienced in life or a particular lifestyle? Shouldn't we all strive to see our experiences from the perspective of Scripture rather than Scripture from the perspective of our own personal experiences and desires?

The poor, desolate, abused, widowed, betrayed, abandoned, afflicted, weary, ignorant, affluent, healthy, educated, comfortable, and strong all have personal experiences that are vastly different from each other. If there was no standard from which to understand and wrestle with these life experiences, then we, of all creatures, would be a most pitiful lot. But there is a single standard. It is the written descriptive and prescriptive word of God. That means that it describes certain truths so that we can know them rightly and it prescribes certain truths so that we will apply them for right living. It is the source from which all understanding of life can come from. Science, art, philosophy, and all other disciplines of study are beautiful tools to use in exploring life and expressing God's glory, but they all need to be founded in the worldview of the biblical Genesis. Let's look at how this affects our reading of Scripture.

A Worldview

If we approach the Bible with the worldview that we are the central characters in the drama of life, then we read the stories of Joseph, Moses, David, Esther, and Ruth as triumphs of human character and faithfulness that we should strive to emulate.

> When we study the character of God as revealed in His Word and then study His Word to see how to reflect that character, we become faithful Image Bearers, not human imitators.

We look to them to see what godly traits they displayed so we can be more like them in faithfulness or stewardship or leadership. These are good humans that God found pleasure in using. But step back for a second. Look and see how drastically the picture changes when we approach with our above-stated worldview drawn from Genesis 1.

Now we approach Scripture from the worldview that *God* is the central character who is at all times sovereign and supreme. Now, the story is not about the good qualities of humans that we should celebrate and strive to emulate, but about the sovereignty and faithfulness of God at all times despite the brokenness of humanity in those individuals. He is always there in the midst of circumstances working all things together for His glory and the blessings of those He has chosen for His purposes.

Wow! What a difference! This is the story that God wants us to read and learn. Joseph got into some hairy predicaments, but God was always present, orchestrating life to fulfill His purposes just as He planned. Moses made some pretty nasty judgment calls, but God remained faithful to His promises and held Moses up. Esther was afraid and weak and of no substantial power politically or physically, but God demonstrated his sovereignty over the life of Israel through her story as opposed to the two most powerful men of her day who could have physically destroyed Israel. Ruth and Boaz were generous and kindhearted, but the book of Ruth is more about God's sovereignty and faithfulness to Naomi and the future of Israel than it is about Ruth. God was displaying His providence while perfectly orchestrating the exact circumstances that would raise King David up to lead Israel for His glory (Naomi was King David's great-great-grandma)!

You see, the story is not about man's faithfulness, but about God's! We don't learn how to bear the Image by studying the good characteristics of men. That only leads to reasoning such as, "What would Joseph do?" or "What did David do in this situation?" When we study the character of God as revealed in His Word and then we study His Word to see how to reflect that character, we become faithful Image Bearers, not human imitators.

Here's the difference. Most of us will never have the opportunity to trust God the way that Joseph is portrayed as trusting God. That's because most of us will never live through as terrible circumstances as Joseph did—sold into slavery by our family, framed for capital crimes by influential people, and put in prison all while living the best we know how to. Most of us will never be called before the ruler of the known world, with our life in the balance, to interpret a dream without any foreknowledge of what the dream is. Talk about trusting God to show up! Therefore, the point isn't to learn how to trust God like Joseph did, it's to understand that God is sovereign and faithful through even the most tragic circumstances, and for that, He can be trusted.

Knowing this then, we as individuals today can say, "I will act upon the truth that God is sovereign and faithful, no matter what happens in my life" (i.e. "even though my parents have decided that they don't love each other anymore. I will not look for blame or give in to depression, because as messed up as this is, it is not out of God's control. I trust that God still has a purpose for my life and He is greater than my fears and doubts").

Or we may be the individuals who experience the constant pressure to be the perfect student or to follow perfectly in the steps of parents who expect us to be what they have always dreamed for us to be, even though it may not be our dream. Through this experience, we can say, "I know that God is sovereign and faithful, and for me to trust means that I can trust that I am not going to ruin my life or my parents' life just because I disappoint myself or my parents. God is big enough to fulfill His purposes through me even if I don't follow the perfect human plan. Whatever I do, I will do for God's glory and trust Him to be in control of everything else."

We may not experience the horrors of Joseph's life, but we may experience fear at levels in our own life that bring us near to our own breaking points. What we believe about God in the midst of these situations allows us to live for Him the way He designed us to as individuals in our own lives. You may be like Hannah (Samuel's mother) who demonstrated her trust in God by spending many extra hours in prayer. I may be like Noah who demonstrated His trust in God by simply pushing forward and doing the best he could understand. Someone else might be like David who demonstrated his trust in God by writing out his fears and doubts in psalms but always ended up praising God in the close of his poetry. As people see the sovereignty and faithfulness of God represented in the way we live out our specific circumstances, they witness the Image Bearing purpose of humanity through each of us in beautifully unique ways!

We then begin to develop a pattern of living and we ask, "Why should I trust God's faithfulness in this?" and, "How should I respond to this specific situation trusting that He is in control of it?" We call this change "spiritual maturity," and we reflect spiritual maturity by bearing our unique reflection of God's Image in us. If we pursue faithful stewardship of the Image of God uniquely in us, we will exhibit those traits we strive to emulate in the saints anyway.

If we wanted to apply this to the way we study the Bible, then a good Bible study would be to study the life of Joseph; a great Bible study would be to study how God used the events of Joseph's life to bring out the traits Peter talks about in 2 Peter 1:3–9 and then discuss where we are in the development of those responsibilities in our own life.

The Genesis Worldview

So let's start with Genesis again and see what it teaches. Since Genesis begins with a theological foundation, we need to ask why it is so important that God starts with this theological account.

We find from the first chapter that God is the ultimate beginning and cause of all of Creation. His power and majesty brought everything into existence simply by speaking it! The very forces of the cosmos and nature exist because He willed them. He decided what was good from the start, and it was so simply because He said so. *His will makes all of creation work!* This is what awesome is! This is sovereignty! God is completely in a class of His own.

And why does He make this apparent at the beginning? Because the very next thing He does brings His glory and majesty into the spotlight. Lest we get lost in the wonder and beauty of His creation, forgetting about the Creator, He creates man! He created man to point creation back to Him as the central character, not to make the man the central character. We know this because Scripture tells us that we were created to bear *His* Image in the midst of all creation. He did this so that His glory would be seen and demonstrated by everything that man, this pinnacle of creation, does.

Scripture tells us that man is created to bear the Image of God and to care for all of creation as a physical steward.

> Then God said, "Let Us make man in Our image, according to Our likeness; and let them rule over the fish of the sea and over the birds of the sky and over the cattle and over all the earth, and over every creeping thing that creeps on the earth." God created man in His own image, in the image of God He created him; male and female He created them.
> God blessed them; and God said to them, "Be fruitful and multiply, and fill the earth, and subdue it; and rule over the fish of the sea and over the birds of the sky and over every living thing that moves on the earth.
>
> Genesis 1:26–28

> When I consider Your heavens, the work of Your fingers,
> The moon and the stars, which You have ordained;
> What is man that You take thought of him,

And the son of man that You care for him?
Yet You have made him a little lower than God,
And You crown him with glory and majesty!
You make him to rule over the works of Your
hands;
You have put all things under his feet,
All sheep and oxen,
And also the beasts of the field,
The birds of the heavens and the fish of the sea,
Whatever passes through the paths of the seas.
O LORD, our Lord,
How majestic is Your name in all the earth!

Psalm 8: 3–9

Many people will stop at the end of chapter one of Genesis, but chapter two is just as important in forming a worldview as chapter one is. Both chapters are part of the same story. The first gives us a God-centered theological look, and the second tells us how man reflected God and how evil originated.

To Bear the Image
Man reflected God. Wow!

Let's discuss what this means for man as he bears the Image of God. Bearing His Image means more than just being like Jesus in form or character. It means that each one of us is given the responsibility to be His representative here on this planet. Think of all the most magnificent things you can imagine: Jupiter in the sky, the sun, a sunset, Mount Everest, the Grand Canyon, the earth itself, the dinosaurs, the great blue whale, the ocean. God did not create any of these things to be his representation on Earth. None of these things were given the responsibility to care for everything else; to make things grow and develop; to rule everything and make it better; to decide how, where, and when things would be; to have meaningful relationships that would affect the rest of creation. Nothing else was crowned with glory and honor. This great responsibility was given to man. Man would be God's physical representation over this small portion of Creation called Earth. Man's ability to do these things is a reflection of His Image. Not the whole Image, but the parts reflected are God's Image and no one else's.

The life of Abraham is a great example of a man learning to steward the Image of God to purposefully glorify God in the specifics of his life. In the beginning chapters of Abram's life in Scripture (Genesis 12–21), we see a man who is more concerned with his own welfare and domestic tranquility than with seeing the manifestation of God's glory in his life. God had promised to bless him and watch after him, blessing those who blessed him and cursing those who cursed him, yet Abram still acted in fear and self-preservation both with foreigners and at home with his family.

But we see a much different Abraham in the final chapters of his life (Genesis 21–25). Abraham had been changed through the trials along his path to be a man that trusted God and pointed to God's glory when the circumstances of life threatened the harmony of his life. His son's life was threatened, his wife died, and he struggled to find a wife for his son as he approached death. In all these matters, however, he learned to point to God's glory with his life. He trusted God. He knew God was good and sovereign. He acted according to that knowledge even when there was no apparent way that in doing so, things would work out the way God said they would.

Abram became Abraham and learned to glorify God through the Image he was given to steward. He used it to point out God's glory.

How does this story help me today? Remember what we talked about above. Our own circumstances will dictate specifically how we point out God's glory with our own lives. It may be strength and peacefulness in the midst of a parents' divorce. It may be courage in the face of a career or life-changing decision. It may be dignity and humility in the pain of a broken relationship. The point is that we reflect God's Image by demonstrating our faith in His sovereignty and faithfulness in whatever way is appropriate for who God made us.

Strength, peacefulness, courage, dignity, and humility are all marks of His Image being represented in us through our faith. It is when we focus on His purpose for our life instead of the brokenness of our circumstances that we experience the power of the Holy Spirit conforming us into the likeness of Christ. This is what it means to be an Image Bearer.

Gifts, Skills, and Responsibilities

Look at the responsibilities God gave to man. He gave him authority to name every creature (2:19). He was responsible for tending to creation—creation needed man to care for it before the fall (2:15)! Finally (and this one is my favorite because it is so liberating and empowering to the common Christian such as myself), man was responsible for taking what was given to him and *making it better* (1:28). Not all of creation was a Garden of Eden. God created a garden in one particular spot and placed man there in order to care for it and ordered him to be fruitful (use the gifts and abilities for the purposes that God intended; remember Psalm 8) and multiply (increase those who would reflect God's glory and bear God's Image)! The whole world was not a Garden of Eden, but God entrusted man to make of it whatever he wanted, because without sin, that could only result in good.

I hope you notice that God gave the same command to all creation, but I believe the command was specific to each creature to fulfill its intended purpose and multiply. The Hebrew translation of "be fruitful and multiply" is a not a single word that means what we have come to join together as a single cliché, "to make babies." They are two different words with two different thoughts. I believe that God was blessing each creature with the empowerment to do what it was supposed to (be fruitful) and also reproduce (multiply).

If God wanted to be redundant, then according to Hebrew poetry, Hebrew use of tropes, and the rest of the Pentateuch, Moses would have simply repeated the same word, said the entire statement again, or used some form of figurative language. That is usually how the Hebrew language of the Old Testament marks repetition in order to make a point. That is not done here. It appears that God intended for two different thoughts to be conveyed. For man, that meant stewarding God's creation, bearing His Image, and bringing God glory through living, working, and making more people to further bear the Image! God is not so concerned with people filling the earth numerically as He is with people filling the earth with His Image in order for His glory to be continually manifested through those He created to be His stewards of Creation.

Just as the living Word spoke all Creation and life into existence, He also spoke purpose into our lives! That purpose is glorifying Him through the good stewardship of what He has given to us, whether it be our body, our mind, our voice, our talents, our work, etc.

This is exciting stuff! It means that life finds purpose in any endeavor, regardless of its stature or acclaim, as long as it glorifies God through doing it well. That was the original purpose of life.

Before sin entered creation, this wasn't a problem. Everything would be done well. Everything Adam and Eve did was glorifying to God. Now of course, we do have to discern if something is a manifestation of God's grace or a manifestation of sin. Choosing to be a country singer or a rock star that sings about the joy of getting high and loose sexual behavior is of course not glorifying of God.

…life finds purpose in any endeavor, regardless of its stature or acclaim, as long as it glorifies God through doing it well. That was the original purpose of life.

Using that same gift of music and singing to celebrate or share in a biblically positive way the many facets of life is.

Is making shoes glorifying of God even though the name of the shoe line is not *Nike Messiah*? How about being a garbage man? Or a pizza maker? Or an auto mechanic? Of course it is! These are all manifestations of God's gift to steward creation through the creativity and the development of given skills. When done well, they are celebrations of what God has given as a quality of an Image Bearer.

Can you imagine what our world would look like if no one took up the responsibility to dispose of waste material properly, if no one could fix a car or mend a dress or wash a skyscraper window? It may seem like a small thing, or you may say, "Yes, but we do that because we have to, not because we are trying to glorify God."

But think back to Adam in the Garden of Eden. Was he commanded to glorify God? No. He was commanded to be fruitful, multiply, and care for the garden. God reveals to us now, after the fact of sin, through the biblical narrative, that His intended purpose was for man to glorify Him. For Adam, it was simply a matter of life. He did what needed to be done because it was his responsibility to do it. *He would do his best at what God gave him to do, and God would be pleased as His glory was made evident by this one reflecting His image.*

It's the same today with anyone who stewards creation in one way or another. Whether he or she intends it or not, glory is given to God when His creatures fulfill any of those commands simply because they bear the Image of God through the responsibility of stewardship. No one will be able to stand before God one day and say in defiance, "I never displayed Your glory!" All of creation and the angels will be able to testify to the stewardship and skills of that individual that were only possible through the Image Bearing quality of humanity. (This does not imply that displaying the Image means salvation; we know that salvation is based on faith in grace through Christ alone. It does, however, mean that

God created man in His Image, not only Christians. In chapter nine, we will see how this influences how we do evangelism!)

It is the same for artful expression. When done well and not as a gratification of sinful expression, it glorifies God through the Image Bearing quality man bears as a fruit-producing steward of that skill. So if you are a garbage man, a poet, a musician, a woodworker, a mechanic, a seamstress, a nurse, or a basketball player, do it well and take pride and joy in it if it becomes a lifetime occupation for you. Realize the liberty given to you in Genesis 1 and 2 to enjoy and celebrate life as a steward and an Image Bearer. There is no shame or disappointment in this part. Your life is about Him! Do you see now how a proper worldview can change your life?

"There is no shame or disappointment in this part."

I hope you caught that in the last paragraph. Human beings are holistic in nature. That means that as we bear the Image of our Creator, we have an emotional, intellectual, social, physical, and spiritual aspect to our being. We are not made to live in a vacuum of one or two of those aspects at the expense of ignoring the others. That does not mean that we *have to be* social butterflies, perfect specimens of fitness, A+ students across the board, steady in our emotions at all times, and awe-inspiring evangelists all at the same time. It does mean that we need to engage life at all levels, not just where we have the most fun.

Think about a time when you have been so overwhelmed with homework or work (even though you love it) that you just wanted to chill out with friends for a bit. Or maybe you've experienced a time in life when you have had to be strong for someone else and not allowed yourself the emotional outlet you needed, when in reality, what you wanted more than anything else was to break down and cry or scream. Or perhaps there has been an instance in your life when you took a break from everything and just treated yourself to a few days of fun only to realize halfway through that you really wanted to "do something" in order to feel productive. These are all examples of the internal struggles we all go through when something is out of balance in those five areas of life.

So strive for balance. Don't allow a single area of your life that you excel in to be an excuse to shirk your responsibility as an Image Bearer in every other area of your life. If you're one of the best basketball players at your school, don't isolate yourself from the community of other human beings who don't share your same interests. If you're a great artist or musician, don't use commitment of time to perfecting your trade as an excuse to not study God's Word. As much as we glorify God in our celebration of the gifts and skills and responsibilities that He has given to us, it is our responsibility to be fruitful in all of life.

God created us to be "alive," not "about."

Being a master of one thing in no way exempts us from being a steward of any other Image trait, such as kindness, faithfulness, gentleness, peacefulness, patience, joy, righteousness, and love.

God created us to be *alive*, not *about*. That means

that He intended for us to enjoy all of life. All of it! He did not intend for us to simply excel at one thing and then drudge through the rest of life "going about" our business or to the other extreme of doing one thing well and partying through the rest of life without notice of our other responsibilities. Life was meant to be rich and meaningful. So don't neglect the rest of your life at the expense of one single pleasure or skill; God has a lot more to offer the world through you!

The Origins of Evil

The second great part of chapter two focuses on the origins of evil. It is very important to learn early on that God did not create evil. Many critics who look to discredit the Bible look at chapter two and, among other things, point out that God is the Creator of all things and therefore must be the Creator of evil; therefore, He cannot be a good God.

Chapter two of Scripture does not teach that evil was created. It shows that evil came about. Evil is not a thing. It does not exist as an entity unto itself. It only exists in the vacuum created by a rejection of God, His sovereignty, or His presence. Evil does not exist any more than cold does. Cold is the absence of heat. Heat exists, but cold does not. We only refer to something as "cold" when heat is absent.

We use the word *cold* to describe the absence of heat. We use the word *evil* to describe the absence of submission to God's rule. People have misused the word *evil* today to apply to anything that is not deemed acceptable by common human standards of right and wrong. For example, someone might say that dancing is evil. That is a reflection of a human standard that has been attached to a human activity. Scripture does not teach that dancing is evil; it teaches that anything that refuses God's presence and sovereignty over itself is evil. Can certain dancing be a manifestation of evil? Most certainly! Especially if it ignores the Image Bearing quality of another human being and ignores the presence and moral law of God by giving footholds to sexual desire through sexual behavior. But dancing in itself is not evil. The term "evil" as presented in Scripture does not refer to the far left spectrum of human standards—it applies to a perversion of God's standards.

What chapter two does teach is that evil is a result of rejecting God's sovereignty and presence. God did not create evil; it was not created at all. It was simply practiced first by Satan and then taught to man by Satan as a way to live. It then became an inescapable reality that man will never cease to practice evil in this life. Again, evil only exists when a created thing rejects the truth of God; it is not some cosmic force.

Genesis chapter two teaches us that it is sufficient to know that the human heart is capable of evil and, once originated, will perpetuate. This is a stark wake-up call to those who blame Satan for every evil in the world. Adam and Eve continued to practice evil on their own long after Satan was gone from their presence. Be very clear on this: If God had destroyed Satan right then and there in the garden, men would still practice evil today. Evil became a part of humanity, and chapters three through five show us exactly how prominently it took hold of human nature.

The first two lessons of Scripture: 1) God is good and sovereign; 2) man was created to be perfect but is not. Something is broken and needs to be fixed. God is the only one who will be able to fix it because: 1) God is good and sovereign; 2) man was created to be perfect but is not. Something is broken and needs to be fixed. Evil has been practiced, and we cannot stop practicing it of our own accord. The Image was created to glorify God. Only Christ can redeem the Image to glorify God purposefully.

Putting It Together

Owning your worldview is a lot deeper than simply having read the Bible and believing in Jesus Christ. When we know what our worldview is and where it starts, then everything else must agree with that worldview somehow before it becomes integrated into our life and faith. If all experiences are sifted through our worldview, then everything else learned will be more than just knowledge, it will be wisdom that transforms and matures and is life-changing.

I am also suggesting that there is only one proper worldview from which to start. That is the one found in Genesis. God is sovereign. He always is and always has been in control. God created everything, including me, for His glory. I am intended to bear His Image—a task and responsibility given only to humanity. And that task is meant to be one of profound joy and fulfillment.

It's not easy though. The world is broken because of evil. It's important to remember that evil is not something God created to frustrate us, and it is not the presence of Satan. The reason that it is so hard to be an Image Bearer all the time is because as broken Image Bearers, we resist the sovereignty and presence of God in many areas of our life. We are completely capable of practicing evil without Satan. What we need is a blue-print to show us how to fit these truths together.

In the next chapter we'll look at how the Bible forms what we call the "metanarrative" and how this metanarrative ultimately becomes God's blueprint for building our worldview.

Metanarrative: God's Blueprint for Viewing Life

Other than the Father turning away from the Son on the cross, I think the most poignant scene found in Scripture is given to us in Job 38–42. If you haven't read it in a while, let me briefly remind you of the story. Job is in the darkest time of his life. We know this because of the worldview with which he enters into the story. Job holds to the belief that God only allows bad to happen to the unjust, and Job knows that he is not unjust. Everything he believes in is about to be challenged as his well-being and fortune are systematically stripped away.

Not long into the saga of Job, we find that he has been crushed physically, emotionally, mentally, intellectually, and socially. What makes this story so great and difficult at the same time is that Job is never crushed spiritually. In the midst of overwhelming loss and confusion, Job cries out to a mighty, sovereign, and holy God. Job had lost all his children, the affections of his wife, all of his wealth, most of his servants, his physical health, and the security of believing that God would only allow bad circumstances to happen to bad people. What makes this story so dramatic is not the seemingly incredible lack of fairness toward Job but the response of God when he finally offers his perspective.

What makes this story so dramatic is not the seemingly incredible lack of fairness toward Job, but the response of God when He finally offers His perspective.

Now if you've already read this story in detail—be fair—what did you think God would say at first? Something along the lines of, "Sorry, Job, but I knew that you would be faithful and strong. I wanted the world to have an example to encourage them through hard times. I will repay you for your faithfulness now, and by the way, well done, my good and faithful servant!" That's what I would've expected at first. It makes sense from a human point of view looking back in 20/20 vision.

But God doesn't say anything like that. He blows us away by presenting a completely different perspective that provides for us the true purpose of this story being preserved. Let me point out a couple of my favorite verses in this part of the narrative:

> Then the LORD answered Job out of the whirlwind and said, "Who is this that darkens my counsel, By words without knowledge?
>
> Job 38: 1–2

> "Will the faultfinder contend with the Almighty? Let him who reproves God answer it."
>
> Job 40:2

"Will you really annul My judgment? Will you
condemn Me that you may be justified?

Job 40:8

Wow! If you read the book of Job and skip chapters
38:1–42:10, you would think that the point of this story is
to display the character of Job and encourage modern-
day saints who are persecuted to endure and be faithful
like Job. The focus would be on Job. But insert God.
Chapters 38–42 reveal that God isn't concerned with the
fairness of Job's situation as much as He is with the perspective that God owes man some kind of answer for the
way things are—a perspective that implies that somehow things got out of control and the supreme God of
creation is not totally sovereign.

God never once answers the question of why this is
happening to Job. He simply reaffirms the sovereignty
that He exercises over all of creation, and lo and behold,
Job is satisfied! He doesn't argue and say to God, "Yeah,
but God, that's not what I asked. Why is this happening to me?" Job simply says, "I opened my mouth once
demanding an answer. I was wrong; I will not do it again"
(paraphrase mine).

What does this have to do with this book? The
Bible is a complete story. It is not a collection of stories put together to encourage the believers; it is a single
story from beginning to end that shows what God has
been doing since the beginning of time concerning his
intended purposes. This big story is what theologians
call the "metanarrative." Knowing how to read the Bible
as a metanarrative is the key to developing the worldview
that God intended to mature our faith and free us to live
the life He intended as His Image Bearers. Like Job, we

need to find within the pages of Scripture a worldview that explains our life experiences, not one that our life experiences can explain.

Our Salvation and God's Glory

In theatrical terms, the Bible has four main acts: the Creation, the Fall, the Redemption, and the Consummation. This brief overview is a synopsis of the metanarrative. Throughout this great drama, God weaves an incredible story of salvation promised to, worked out, and delivered to man.

The Gospel story is the most awesome and mind-shattering story ever told. But the Gospel story is not focused on the salvation of man—it is focused on the goodness and glory of God. That is why the psalmist declares in Psalm 78:7 that the purpose of his teachings is so generations would "put their confidence in God and not forget God's works, but keep His commandments." Every time we read about the history of God and man's relationship in Scripture, we need to remember that God and man began with a trusting relationship in Creation. That is where we find His purpose and intention for Creation, not after the Fall. That puts a lot of stake in the first few pages of Scripture. We need to understand it before we move to the Fall, the Redemption, and then the Consummation.

For example, if we were to take a survey of what God's single most important agenda is, we would probably come up with a variety of answers. Some people might answer that God's number one agenda is the salvation of lost souls. Some might reply that it is peace and unity. Some people might argue that God's greatest concern is the social justice or liberty of all men. While all of these are works that God is accomplishing and will ultimately fulfill according to His will, they are only peripheral benefits to the all-time number one agenda of God Almighty: the glorification of the Father by uplifting the name of Jesus Christ in the power of the Holy Spirit! That's right; God's number one agenda is the glory of God!

Where do we find this? In the first chapter of Scripture, and then if we pay attention, we see it reiterated throughout all Scripture. But don't get caught up in the deception that God is self-centered in the way that human beings are. His self-centeredness gives purpose to life, freedom to the captive, and life, love, and unity to the Church.

> When we begin to view the world through the perspective that everything we do in it and everything He does in it is intended to bring Him glory, then life suddenly becomes much more meaningful and rewarding.

It's interesting to note that apart from describing the Last Supper, Paul the apostle never quotes Jesus directly in any of his Epistles. Again, except for the Last Supper, Paul makes no mention of any of the events of Christ's life apart from crucifixion. From reading Paul alone, you would never know that Jesus taught in parables, performed any miracles, or that He was born of a virgin birth.[1]

Why is this? Probably because Paul wanted to emphasize God's main agenda over and above the peripheral benefits that come with that main agenda. Paul's message to his readers is over and over again the incredible mystery of a God who offers grace and peace to His creation for their salvation to His glory! In Paul's life, the main goal was always God's glory. In fact, if God's main purpose were the salvation of man, we wouldn't even know about Paul—the Bible would end at the Gospel's revelation of the resurrection of Christ. Everything after is discipling instruction for the stewardship of the faith delivered in the Gospel story in order to glorify God.

Reading and teaching God's story as He meant for it to be read becomes a very serious responsibility when we begin to look at every act as it pertains to the number one agenda of God. When we begin to view the world through the perspective that everything we do in it and everything He does in it is intended to bring Him glory, then life suddenly becomes much more meaningful and rewarding. Here is the kicker, though: Life is not more meaningful and rewarding simply because it is intended to glorify God but because everything you do is intended to glorify God! It's the fact that you were created so that anything you do can be glorifying to God.

I look around the room that I sit in as I write this, and I see the effects of God's Image Bearers. I see a highlighter lying next to a pack of Tic Tacs. I see my DVD player and a book that I read to my one-year-old a couple of hours ago. I also see a notebook in which I keep all my plans and schedule, along with a camera and a calculator. Next to my rack, I see my boots and my Bible. All of these items are products of the ingenuity and labor of some Image Bearer whom I will never meet. Would it be fair of me to think that the first of these individuals whom I will meet at eternity's welcome mat will be the person who was responsible for printing and publishing my Bible? Is there any real reason to think that I would meet that person at all, more than any of the others responsible for those other products? I don't think so. God gave His Image Bearers the responsibility to take life by the reins and make it better. The quality of my life is better because others had the passion to make their beneficial ideas realities.

Nephla is a great example of a human being bearing the Image of God. Nephla is a dish that my mother makes using milk, butter, dumplings, butter, potatoes, and butter. I'm pretty sure that God did not create nephla. Come to think of it, he probably didn't make bread either, though he did make wheat. I'm pretty certain that bread and nephla taste a lot better than straight wheat kernels! It was some wonderful human being somewhere that used his or her God-given creativity and created nephla for me to enjoy! (Notice that that sentence still points back to God as the ultimate giver and creator and the only one worthy of praise.)

That is what I mean when I say that God intended for man to make creation better. He was to experience life in the Garden of Eden and then make all of Creation, where the garden wasn't, better. There was an eternity of growing, organizing, designing, and nurturing to do and creative ingenuity to apply. Without the presence of sin, it could only get better through man being an Image Bearer.

This means that the world you live in stands to benefit from your unique gifts and abilities if you live purposefully as an Image Bearer for Christ. Pursue the desires God has given you. Steward and develop the talents and gifts He has given you. Create, build, design, work, sing, dance, write, think, share, serve, do, and love. The world will benefit and be better because of how God manifests His Image in you.

Creation Versus the Fall

If we read the Bible as if God's purpose and plan for us began at the fall, then we miss the glorious design for our own lives. God wants to delight in us. He wants the rest of Creation to delight in us. Sin has made a mess of things, and things will never again be the same; however, that does not mean that we should read Scripture as if it began with the Fall.

Think about the implications of this. What would have happened if Adam and Eve had never sinned? Would their ultimate goal have been to die and go to heaven? Think about the answer before you continue. The answer is no. There would have been no death and therefore no provision for any other "home" than the one Genesis, chapters one and two, gives them, namely, Earth.

> If we read the Bible as if God's purpose and plan begin at the fall, then we miss the glorious design for our own lives.

What does that tell us about the purpose of heaven and the literal new earth? What about marriage? What should marriage look like in light of Creation and not the Fall? What should the church look like? What should evangelism look like? Depending on where your worldview begins, your answers may be very different.

If we begin with the Fall, most ministries become man-centered in order to promote the welfare of man through salvation, justice, peace, or miracles. If we start with Creation though, everything we do or are involved in becomes a ministry to others for the purpose of exhibiting God's glory: marriage, work, fellowship, prayer, encouragement, play, service, gift sharing, skill sharing, etc. We still reap the benefits of redemption along the way, but God becomes the central focus again.

This is the blueprint that God provides for us as we approach the daily task of making decisions to live for God's glory. This is the blueprint for living life. We don't have to agonize over the choices He has given us in order to decide which decision will glorify Him; the glory is made manifest in living the life, if the decision is to live it for Him by taking pleasure in it and doing it well, according to His will. That means fulfilling the Creator's command to be fruitful stewards of this creation should free us to find joy and personal fulfillment in any physical, mental, social, and emotional journey that we undertake as long as we live according to His will. We will get to what "according to His will" means in the next chapter.

For now we can contemplate reading the metanarrative with the proper worldview.

It's Harder Than Christians Sometimes Give It Credit For

Every blueprint has a technical aspect. Not everyone can walk up to a blueprint and make sense of what they see. It takes specific training and the ability to translate what we see in symbols and numbers into a finished structure. The worldview is our "structure," and the metanarrative is our "blueprint."

Scripture is so rich and full and all encompassing of

life that it is hard to imagine how anyone other than God could be credited with its creation! There are, within its pages, the principles and fundamental guidance to all of life's joys and sorrows. It teaches us how to find the joys that God intends for us, how to avoid the world's substitute for true joy, and how to handle the sorrow that comes from living in a broken world. Scripture tells us how to handle joys and sorrows if they find us unexpectedly, and it tells us what to expect if we choose the wrong ones willfully. I cannot think of a situation in my life or in the life of the history of man as I know it that cannot be dealt with according to the principles laid out in Scripture. I am confident that there never will arise such an event or occasion. However, I know, as every believer does, that it is sometimes difficult to find the direction I seek for everyday life.

God's blueprint reveals to us, as it did to Job, that no matter what happens in life, He is faithful to His agenda and faithful to His promises. The problem that we sometimes run into is that we expect God to be faithful to His promise to us, but we don't want to see every situation through until His glory is manifest. Once again, if we choose to think through Scripture as it relates to us and view it as a book of promises to give us encouragement through life, then we miss the primary purpose of the story. My ability to read Scripture with the proper perspective comes through study and maturity. It is not a natural inborn ability automatically activated upon redemption. We will get to this in chapter six.

> My ability to read Scripture with the proper perspective in mind comes through study and maturity. It is not a natural inborn ability automatically activated upon redemption.

You think you've heard this before. You're right. You think you've applied it. Maybe. Let's look at a few things.

Are you in a broken relationship with your parents or siblings because you view your pride or righteous position in the argument as more important than God's glory? Are you involved in sexual behavior outside of marriage because you choose personal gratification over God's glory? Do you celebrate in horror films, violent video games, or pornography rather than forsaking them for his glory? Do you talk about other people or groups of people, such as women, minorities, or homosexuals, in a dehumanizing manner rather than with grace for God's glory? How about your job? Do you complain about your job and belittle those above or below you through your words and actions, or do you live your life for God's glory? At church, do you gossip about others around your Sunday school table or shun those who don't act the way you think they should, or do you glorify God through being a member of the same body?

Knowing that God's glory is paramount is one thing. Applying it to everything is difficult because we live in a broken world. Even our churches are made up of broken, fallen human beings. We need to know how to read the blueprints correctly so we can give it our best educated effort.

Putting It Together

Throughout all of God's revelation and the story of His plan through the Bible, one thing remains the same at all times. It is not the character of man but the sovereignty and glory of God. There is nothing in the pages of this book, which in context, does not point back to this truth. This is God's greatest revelation to mankind and our greatest assurance of the hope that has been promised to us. All things rest in His sovereignty and ultimately work out for His glory.

The blueprint points me toward reading God's Word from the perspective of God working in and through our lives for His glory. The ability to approach life from this perspective is not natural for fallen human beings; we have to work at living life this way and reading His word from this perspective. It takes time, training, and maturity for this to become a lifestyle habit.

So now that we know what God's main agenda is (His own glory), and now that we know His intended perspective on life (life is intended to be an expression of God's glory through whatever we do or He does), what do we do with it? We read and allow ourselves to be transformed through a new way of thinking! If you have not been able to find peace in the journey, this is where the joy of living begins.

God's Will:
Hebrews 13:20–21

I am convinced that the will of God is perceived as a very mysterious thing in the modern-day church. I say that because people seem to go about "finding it" in almost every conceivable manner. I don't believe that it is supposed to be viewed that way.

I've read a great book by Dr. Gary Meadors titled Decision Making God's Way that points out the importance of making God-honoring decisions based on the will of God as it is already revealed to us through God's Word. All of us can live without anxiety of angering God (as long as we make choices according to what is revealed in His word) because the will of God, as far as we will ever need to know it, is already revealed to us in whole.

God's will is not a "take-some-as-you-need-it" guidance counselor who waits to give you what you need until you come to Him and ask for it. It does not need to be accessed by prayer and fasting and waiting. These are tools for discernment of how to best apply what I know God's will to be, not how to find it. You already know God's will as far as He wants you to know it. God's will is already revealed in His Word. The will of God is the instruction for living (loving, sharing, caring, serving, doing, being, studying, discipling, and enduring) that we find in the Bible. It's the same for every person, but our individual design for bearing His Image will manifest His will in different ways as we pursue our own relationship with Him.

Are there specifics in your individual, day-to-day life in which you need to seek guidance through prayer and meditation of Scripture? Certainly. Are there major decisions in your life that require prayer and reflection on God's Word? Absolutely. But the key in these situations is that prayer and meditation refer you back to God's already complete guidance. We have everything we need already available to us in order to make God-honoring decisions as set forth in His moral standards and expressed purpose for life (His glory). Seeking God's direction in our lives should lead us back to our starting point (Scripture), not to some external sign or signal.

> Therefore be careful how you walk, not as unwise men but as wise, making the most of your time, because the days are evil. So then do not be foolish, but understand what the will of the LORD is.
>
> Ephesians 5: 15–17

Ephesians is an interesting book. Paul doesn't mention any specific crisis or heresy that he is exhorting the brethren to overcome. Ephesians seems to be more of a personal letter to help the Christians in Ephesus understand what God's eternal purposes and goals are for the Church.

In Ephesians 3:3–4 Paul makes a very simple statement that sets up what follows. Regarding the revelation that was given to Paul that he teaches in his writings, Paul states, "By reading this you are able to understand my insight about the mystery of the Messiah." Paul then goes on through the rest of the letter to teach how to live like Christ in the unity of the Spirit. Don't miss this. Paul is telling the church in Ephesus what God's big picture purpose is and what He wants from His Church.

Paul refers to his own teachings and other knowledge the Ephesians already possess in telling them not to be foolish but to know what the Lord's will is.

> He made known to us the mystery of His will, according to His kind intention which He purposed in Him with a view to an administration suitable to the fullness of the times, that is, the summing up of all things in Christ, things in the heavens and things on the earth.
>
> Ephesians 1:9–10

Paul then goes on through the rest of the letter to teach how to live like Christ in the unity of the Spirit. Don't miss this! Paul is telling the Church in Ephesus what God's big picture purpose is and what God wants from His Church. Paul is teaching the Ephesians about being mature in the understanding that *they already have.*

> But you did not learn Christ in this way, if indeed you have heard Him and have been taught in Him, just as truth is in Jesus, that, in reference to your former manner of life, you

lay aside the old self, which is being corrupted in accordance with the lusts of deceit, and that you be renewed in the spirit of your mind, and put on the new self, which in the likeness of God has been created in righteousness and holiness of the truth.

Ephesians 4:20–24

According to 4:20–24 then, this knowledge should enable them and encourage them to be Image Bearers (God's will for them) by putting off the old and putting on the new (the how) in order to please God by imitating Christ. Again in chapter 5, Paul says:

Therefore be imitators of God, as beloved children; and walk in love, just as Christ also loved you and gave Himself up for us, an offering and a sacrifice to God as a fragrant aroma. But immorality or any impurity or greed must not even be named among you, as is proper among saints; and there must be no filthiness and silly talk, or coarse jesting, which are not fitting, but rather giving of thanks. For this you know with certainty, that no immoral or impure person or covetous man, who is an idolater, has an inheritance in the kingdom of Christ and God.

Ephesians 5:1–5

Paul fully expected his readers to be able to understand the will of the Lord simply by referring to the knowledge they already had as it had been revealed by God in Jesus Christ through the teaching of the apostles and prophets. The skill they needed to exercise, according to 5:15–17, is not a prayerful petition asking for more revelation, but wisdom to apply what is already laid out before them.

> Pay careful attention, then, to how you walk—not as unwise people but as wise—making the most of the time, because the days are evil. So don't be foolish, but understand what the Lord's will is.
>
> Ephesians 5:15–17

Seeking God's direction in our lives should lead us back to our starting point (Scripture), not to some external sign or signal.

I don't think that waiting a set period of time to make major life decisions is bad. It may be very necessary to give yourself time to think through all the implications of making a certain decision. That's just being a good steward and applying some practical wisdom. Time may give you the opportunity to consider things that you wouldn't have thought of if forced to make an immediate call.

For example, if I were offered a job to go back to the military for another year, some of the immediate considerations I have are the great medical benefits, the good pay as an officer, the adventure, the job security, the free housing. Some of the downsides are the possibility of deploying without my family again, the possibility of my wife and sons having to experience my death, the need to move, having to see or experience things people weren't made to see or experience, limited health care options for family members, 24/7 work schedules, physical fitness standards that have to be maintained, working with and for people I may not wish to, etc. I'm not saying that prayer is simply a means to think more clearly; rather, my prayer time is focused on centering my decisions on God's moral guidelines and asking for proper perspective.

Giving myself time to think about it with my wife, though, is not so much waiting for God to give me an answer as it is giving myself time to consider other effects such as leaving behind friends, the impact on future goals, family, and support networks. It may also involve my wife's career never taking off or my children not being able to grow up in the environment that my wife and I desire. I may have not considered the inability to serve on mission trips anymore if I didn't give myself time to think.

The main point, though, is that no matter what I decide, God is no less glorified. What determines his approval of my decision is whether or not I am making a decision that supports his already revealed moral standards, then the way that I live out that decision, either to his glory or not. How many people agonize over making decisions because they think that God has presented them with several options only as if to say, "Choose wisely now, because only one is the decision I want you to make. You'll be punished if you choose the wrong option." There is no precedent in Scripture of God being that kind of a manipulating Father. God does not offer bad options. He does not tempt us with evil. He only gives us good so that we may bear His Image better.

Let no one say when he is tempted, "I am being tempted by God"; for God cannot be tempted by evil, and He Himself does not tempt anyone. But each one is tempted when he is carried away and enticed by his own lust. Then when lust has conceived, it gives birth to sin; and when sin is accomplished, it brings forth death. Do not be deceived, my beloved brethren. Every good thing given and every perfect gift is from above, coming down from the Father of lights, with whom there is no variation or shifting shadow. In the exercise of His will He brought us forth by the word of truth, so that we would be a kind of first fruits among His creatures.

James 1:13–18

You want to work in Dallas? Work in Dallas. You want to work in Chicago? Work in Chicago. You want to lay bricks? Lay bricks. You want to be a sales rep for a major firm? Go ahead. You want to go to this school over that one even though that one is a private Christian university and this one is not? At the heart of the matter is what you intend to do with that choice. Will you pursue the world and its image, or will you use that decision to pursue God's glory through your Image Bearing? Your choice for either of two options will not bring you in line with God's will so much as the way you live your life in the midst of that choice.

You have God's will in front of you in Scripture. As long as your choices reflect that guidance, God will use you and move you to the glory of His name. Let's look at what the Apostle Peter teaches.

Simon Peter, a bond-servant and apostle of Jesus Christ, To those who have received a faith of the same kind as ours, by the righteousness of our God and Savior, Jesus Christ:

Grace and peace be multiplied to you in the knowledge of God and of Jesus our Lord; seeing that His divine power has granted to us everything pertaining to life and godliness, through the true knowledge of Him who called us by His own glory and excellence.

For by these He has granted to us His precious and magnificent promises, so that by them you may become partakers of the divine nature, having escaped the corruption that is in the world by lust.

Now for this very reason also, applying all diligence, in your faith supply moral excellence, and in your moral excellence, knowledge, and in your knowledge, self-control, and in your self-control, perseverance, and in your perseverance, godliness, and in your godliness, brotherly kindness, and in your brotherly kindness, love. For if these qualities are yours and are increasing, they render you neither useless nor unfruitful in the true knowledge of our Lord Jesus Christ. For he who lacks these qualities is blind or short-sighted, having forgotten his purification from his former sins.

Therefore, brethren, be all the more diligent to make certain about His calling and closing you; for as long as you practice these things, you will never stumble; for in this way the entrance into the eternal kingdom of our Lord and Savior Jesus Christ will be abundantly supplied to you.

2 Peter 1:1–11

Peter lays out a very critical piece of guidance for those who wish to grow as disciples of Christ. If you want to walk through life knowing that God is pleased with your life, then focus on the growth of Christ-like character in the midst of life, not on positions, postures, or places that have nothing to do with how you live in those circumstances.

What?

Jesus was once asked, "Of all the commandments, which is the most important?"[2] It is interesting to note Jesus's answer and then the verbal exchange immediately following. Jesus responds with this:

Jesus answered, "The foremost is, 'HEAR, O ISRAEL! THE LORD OUR GOD IS ONE LORD; AND YOU SHALL LOVE THE LORD YOUR GOD WITH ALL YOUR HEART, AND WITH ALL YOUR SOUL, AND WITH ALL YOUR MIND, AND WITH ALL YOUR STRENGTH.' The second is this, 'YOU SHALL LOVE YOUR NEIGHBOR AS YOURSELF.' There is no other commandment greater than these."

Mark 12:29–31

The scribe who asks the question responds with:

> The scribe said to Him, "Right, Teacher; You have truly stated that HE IS ONE, AND THERE IS NO ONE ELSE BESIDES HIM; AND TO LOVE HIM WITH ALL THE HEART AND WITH ALL THE UNDERSTANDING AND WITH ALL THE STRENGTH, AND TO LOVE ONE'S NEIGHBOR AS HIMSELF, is much more than all burnt offerings and sacrifices."
>
> Mark 12:32–33

Jesus makes this awesome statement that begs us to look more closely at what the scribe has just said to Jesus: "You are not far from the kingdom of God" (Mark 12:34).

Why was Jesus so impressed with the scribe's response? Because the scribe rightly suggested that God wasn't satisfied with the burnt offerings of the Jews. They were never intended to bring lasting peace between God and man. Only Christ's death would do that once and for all time. The scribe did not know about Jesus's death obviously, but he did know what Peter would state many years later in his aforementioned letter: God wanted people to do His will in the first place instead of having to offer sacrifices for not having done it. The scribe was demonstrating, as Peter did, that God had already given us what was necessary to live a life pleasing to Him.

Note that these requirements have to do with individual behavior, not national. This implies that people already knew everything that they needed to know about God's will. The scribe was talking about the will of God.

Summed up here very simply: To love Him and to love each other. Perhaps the only other thing needed to bring this man fully into the kingdom now was a faith in Jesus Christ as the Son of God.

The scribe knew God's will and so did all the Israelites, even way back then. God had already given as much of His will as he needed and wanted to give to mankind. Peter knew this reality had been perfected in the death of his Lord.

Today, those born of the Spirit can live a life free from the bondage of sin and free from the darkness that is ignorance of God's will. We don't have to wonder what pleases God or what is necessary for salvation. We know the story of God creating man, man falling into sin and not being able to free himself from it, Christ redeeming us through His death and resurrection, and having everlasting life to look forward to in the New Creation. As far as knowing God's will for our lives, we have it all! Nothing more is needed.

So, that's it?

So, is that it? Can I read the Bible once and put it back, confident that I have all the parables, analogies, and character references I need to make any decision in life according to God's will? I hope you are already thinking, "No, that's absurd." You're right; it is absurd. Peter says in the passage below:

> Now for this very reason also, applying all diligence, in your faith supply moral excellence, and in your moral excellence, knowledge, and in your knowledge, self-control, and in your self-control, perseverance, and in your

perseverance, godliness, and in your godliness, brotherly kindness, and in your brotherly kindness, love. For if these qualities are yours and are increasing, they render you neither useless nor unfruitful in the true knowledge of our Lord Jesus Christ. For he who lacks these qualities is blind or short-sighted, having forgotten his purification from his former sins. Therefore, brethren, be all the more diligent to make certain about His calling and choosing you; for as long as you practice these things, you will never stumble;

2 Peter 1:5–10

Notice the words that are in italics: supplement, increasing, make every effort to confirm. Becoming the skilled blueprint reader that we talked about in the last chapter is not intended to be an overnight process. Spiritual maturity is not intended to be a "phase-of-life" experience. It is intended to be a lifelong journey that needs constant maintenance. God has given us everything we need, but we also need to continue to mature in our understanding and our perspective. We will not be perfect in either until we are raised again in His glory.

You have probably heard something like this before, but the spiritual walk is a lifelong journey broken down into a thousand days of responsibility. Our responsibility is to be "transformed by the renewing of our minds so that we may discern what is the good pleasing and perfect will of God" (Romans 12:2). This doesn't just happen; we have to pursue it through a life of faith and scriptural diet.

The Great Symphony

Spiritual maturity is not intended to be a "phase-of-life" experience. It is intended to be a lifelong journey that needs constant maintenance.

I love symphonies, a thousand sounds blended together in perfect timing to produce harmony and structure. The church is like a great symphony. God has brought millions of people together at just the right times in their lives so that they can glorify him through the life that they live individually and in community.

For those times in life when discernment seems a little harder than just reading God's Word and praying, you have an incredible asset at your disposal. Think about it! You have not only a group of people that know the Word of God and have a relationship with Him from which to seek guidance on your behalf, but they also know you! What an incredible combination! God makes this incredible being that is completely unique and a true one-of-a-kind (you) and then puts you in a place where other people can grow with you and know you and all your uniqueness in order to help you live your life to the fulfillment of what you were created for. The only other relationship that comes close to this and actually surpasses it is marriage.

If you are truly in a spot in life where God's will seems hidden from you, then Scripture, prayer, and the community of the saints should all affirm for you a way for you to go. They always work together, and since the Holy Spirit is the author of all three of these, the answers will be made clear when all three agree.

Community is a two-way street, though. If you want people to know you, then you have to offer yourself to the relationship and allow people to get to know you. Don't always be an observer of the symphony, get in there and play so that when you need it, it is there for you, and so that when you are needed, you are there to be called on.

Peace, Love, and Unity

If I had to sum up the whole of God's will for our lives, I would say this: To glorify God through peace, love, and unity is at the center of the will of God. Christ gave us the two greatest commandments: To love God and to love each other. At the center of these is the message that we find purposed and lived out in the Creation account: peace, love, and unity.

This could easily be mishandled and taken out of a biblical worldview and presented from a postmodern or even 1960s worldview. But the biblical version of peace, unity, and love does not look like the all-embracing methodology of postmodernism, nor does it look like the irresponsible, self-destructive behavior of the 60s forward. Do you see why it is so important to have a properly founded worldview? If we long to live the will of God in our lives, it must begin in our individual lives, then our family lives, then our church community and public lives, striving for peace, unity, and love.[3]

At the personal level, I believe that God desires us to find purpose first in Him. This means that your purpose in life is not in making perfect grades, or fulfilling what you think your parents' expectations are, or being the person you think your boyfriend or girlfriend wants you to be. It means finding peace with the fact that God made you … you. He didn't make you the most popular person in the world, or the best looking, or the best athlete, or most gifted singer. He made you who you are. Being at peace and unity on a personal level means trusting God that He knew what He was doing when He made you. It means pursuing life as you and loving Him for it.

Do you love God for who He made you? Maybe you have put a little too much of those other things in the way of your view of who you are, and now it's time to start peeling away and figuring out whom that really is. Are you ready for that? Are you ready to be happy with God as He reveals you to be and not someone else? He is.

What about the family level? This is a little easier to see but sometimes hard to work out. Are you living at peace with your family? Do you live in unity with them through respect for who they are in relation to you and God? Do you love your family through all the idiosyncrasies that make them your family, or do you resent them for those?

What does God say about love? That if you say you love Him but hate your brother, you are a liar (1 John 4:20). Remember that love is the common theme in the two greatest commandments. It is not an option. It is also given the highest pedestal in 1 Corinthians 13, above faith and hope. Does your home operate in peace, love, and unity? If not, do you strive for it?

I would offer that if you are not striving to achieve these first two realities in your life, then you are already short of where you need to be in order to discern what is the good, pleasing, and perfect will of God (Romans 12:2). Remember that God created life for a purpose, on purpose. It is not a small thing to Him if you live in broken relationships with an apathetic attitude. His desire is for His glory to be made manifest within a broken world by His Image reflecting something drastically different than the brokenness around us.

Finally, peace, unity, and love are supposed to be staples of the community of saints. See if you can see the emphasis on these three foundations from a biblical worldview in these verses. John says this:

> I was very glad to find some of your children walking in truth, just as we have received commandment to do from the Father. Now I ask you, lady, not as though I were writing to you a new commandment, but the one which we have had from the beginning, that we love one another. And this is love, that we walk according to His commandments This is the commandment, just as you have heard from the beginning, that you should walk in it.
>
> 2 John 4–6

Check out what Paul says:

> Do not lie to one another, since you laid aside the old self with its evil practices, and have put on the new self who is being renewed to a true knowledge according to the image of the One who created him—a renewal in which there is no distinction between Greek and Jew, circumcised and uncircumcised, barbarian, Scythian, slave and freeman, but Christ is all, and in all.
>
> Colossians 3:9–11

There are books written on all of these topics. My purpose here is not to expound on the characteristics of a Christ-centered "purpose-driven church" but to show that living out God's will begins at a personal level and daily pierces our lives at every level. If you want to invest in your spiritual maturity as it reflects knowing the will of God, then you need to begin living it at these levels so that when you need help discerning it over major decisions in life, it has already become a lifestyle, not simply a "lifeline."

Putting It Together

God's will is not an illusive, mysterious treasure that all men seek. It is a purpose given to all men freely through the revealed Word of God. It is complete and powerful enough to accomplish any task or purpose set before us in life. All we need to do is look.

It takes work, though. We build upon our understanding of God's will every day through study and application. It takes time, a lifetime, to get it perfect. But when we live in the community that he intended, when we live out the will of God daily on a personal level, and when we rely on and study the Word of God through prayer, it begins to take hold of our lives and transform us into new creations. This is part of what it means to bear the Image. This is what it means to be free. Let's look at that next.

Liberty In Christ:
Living In Christ

I want to begin this chapter with the opening remarks of one of my former pastors in a sermon taken from I Corinthians 10.

> On our study on "Liberty in Christ," we use the term "Liberty in Christ" rather than "Christian Liberty" because some have adopted this idea of Christian liberty to mean somehow that we have inherent rights because of our status as a Christian to do what we want because our security is already settled. That's a really wrong understanding of what Christian liberty is. Our liberty in Christ emphasizes our identity with Him, and our freedom from sin, to be like Him and to bring glory to God and to serve others; to embrace the cross and to live for God's glory.
>
> Pastor Doug Crawford
> West Cannon Baptist Church, Bellmont, MI,
> 25 June 2006

This chapter is about understanding two key theological principles necessary for maturity in our faith: our liberty in Christ and our freedom from sin.

Liberated

In order to fully grasp the idea of Christian liberty we need to begin with what it means to be "freed from the slavery of sin." What does it means to be truly free? The world does not understand how true liberty can come through submission to authority. But when that authority is the perfect righteous wisdom of the Creator who designed life and gave it purpose, submission to that authority is the only act that can bring freedom for the fulfillment of purpose in life.

The world has a different perspective on freedom than the Creator does. The world wants to assert that true freedom is the ability to do what we want without restriction and without retribution. But Paul tells us in Romans 6:23 that "the wages of sin is death, but the gift of God is eternal life through Jesus Christ our Lord." This is a favorite of Christians who like to quote Scripture, but it is interesting to note that most people could probably not tell you what context this verse falls into.

In verses 12 through 22, Paul is making the point that unless we are able to identify with the righteousness of Christ, we are slaves to sin, unable to produce fruit. The consequence of this life apart from the righteousness of Christ is lawlessness and death (verses 19, 21). But to be freed from the reign of sin (verse 12) is to be liberated and enabled to produce fruit (verse 22). Therefore, true freedom is to be freed from the inability to do what God desires (which ends in death) and to be given the ability to do what God desires through His Spirit according to the righteousness of Christ.

This is what it means to be free! I can finally, willfully, obey God and give Him glory by the Spirit through Christ! Before Christ came into this life, there was only sin and the future consequence of death.

Spiritual freedom has come to mean a lot of different things over time, but the purpose of Christ's liberating righteousness credited to us is not to allow us to live life without responsibility, but to give God glory through the righteous living of that responsibility which we are given. The world does not understand how true freedom can come through submission to authority. But when that authority is the perfect righteous wisdom of the Creator who designed life and gave it purpose, submission to that authority is the only act that can bring freedom for the fulfillment of purpose in life. Only a person who has experienced that type of freedom can understand it.

> Now we have received, not the spirit of the world, but the Spirit who is from God, so that we may know the things freely given to us by God, which things we also speak, not in words taught by human wisdom, but in those taught by the Spirit, combining spiritual thoughts with spiritual words. But a natural man does not accept the things of the Spirit of God, for they are foolishness to him; and he cannot understand them, because they are spiritually

appraised. But he who is spiritual appraises all things, yet he himself is appraised by no one.

1 Corinthians 2: 12–15

Liberty

Now we have to deal with this notion of Christian liberty, or, as it has been reframed, liberty in Christ. Since we are freed from bondage in sin to the liberty of righteousness in Christ, how does that liberty work out in our lives? We need to, once again, begin with the main agenda of God. Liberty in Christ is about using the knowledge we have about what God's will is to make confident decisions in living life as Image Bearers so that we may glorify Him.

Liberty has nothing to do with inappropriate behavior from a believer. In fact, liberty in Christ only becomes apparent in our lives when we strive to live for God appropriately.

One of the first temptations we have to fight is the tendency to view our liberty in Christ as a reward for having been saved by grace. As though we Christians have done something so meritorious in God's eyes that we deserve a "get out of jail free" pass. "We don't have to worry about sinning because grace abounds to us." We know this is not true. Sin is sin, and unfortunately, we will all struggle as sinners until the day that we die.

Liberty has nothing to do with inappropriate behavior from a believer. In fact, liberty in Christ only becomes

—————————————— A.M. Lamouria

apparent in our lives when we strive to live for God appropriately. Christian liberty is something we experience more than it is something we demonstrate. The false assumption in not having to worry about sinning is that we put the emphasis of liberty on our behavior. The emphasis should be on the righteousness of Christ.

Putting the emphasis on the righteousness of Christ does two things for us: It frees us from the fear of having failed the requirements of perfect holiness, and it allows us to live among and serve others who do not fully share our worldview. Let's look at an example of each.

Even though we have experienced the saving grace of God through faith in Jesus Christ, many of us still struggle with the insecurity of performance. As broken human beings, we feel that we have to make up for our failures to God somehow by doing something, being better, or acting holier. It's here that we need to remember while God desires for us to conform to the likeness of Christ, failing does not negate the grace of God.

Liberty in Christ frees us from having to beat ourselves up every time we fall. This is why I say that liberty is something we experience more than something we demonstrate and why liberty is really only experienced as we strive to live for God. For it is only in the struggle against our own sinful nature that we find the gracious relief which liberty in Christ provides for us. If we think of liberty as a license to live in sin, then we will find no relief from guilt and shame when we need it most. If we have never understood that liberty frees us from sin-guilt rather than giving us license to sin, then we will never know the comfort of liberty in Christ. It is in our darkest hours when shame and guilt and hopelessness overwhelm us that we question what life is all about. It is then that we most desperately need to understand what liberty truly is.

Romans 1 tells us that everyone recognizes good from evil. The difference between the saved and the unsaved is that the lost suppress the truth and celebrate their depravity. Later on in Romans 7, Paul identifies the inner struggle that we all experience against our own evil thoughts and desires as saved individuals.

> For I know that nothing good dwells in me, that is, in my flesh; for the willing is present in me, but the doing of the good is not. For the good that I want, I do not do, but I practice the very evil that I do not want. But if I am doing the very thing I do not want, I am no longer the one doing it, but sin which dwells in me. I find then the principle that evil is present in me, the one who wants to do good. For I joyfully concur with the law of God in the inner man, but I see a different law in the members of my body, waging war against the law of my mind and making me a prisoner of the law of sin which is in my members.
>
> Romans 7:18–23

The benefit that we have, however, is that we can rely on God's grace to continue its transforming work in us until the day of completion when we are resurrected with Him. That is liberty in Christ! To live free of fear from the inability to stop sinning while striving to become more like Christ, not to celebrate in sin and embrace it.

The second thing that liberty allows is the opportunity for me to operate in a world that is not sterile from sin or opposing worldviews. Could you imagine if God mandated that once we became Christians we had to avoid all parts of Creation that are affected by sin? Obviously, that would leave us no place to live. Liberty acknowledges the inability to escape "taintedness" and gives us the freedom to live in a world where others, Christians and non-Christians, may not subscribe to the exact same worldview we do. In other words, we can't attain perfection in this life. Even if we could, the imperfect world we live in would throw a monkey wrench into our plans somewhere.

So don't beat yourself or anybody else up for not being what you perceive to be "perfection driven." Enjoy life as an Image Bearer in community with other Image Bearers encouraging one another and building each other up. Freedom in Christ liberates all of us from having to attain perfection on our own. Perfection can only be found in Christ. Paul speaks to this in Romans 14:1–12 and then again in 1 Corinthians 10:23–33.

> Now accept the one who is weak in faith, but not for the purpose of passing judgment on his opinions. One person has faith that he may eat all things, but he who is weak eats vegetables only. The one who eats is not to regard with contempt the one who does not eat, and the one who does not eat is not to judge the one who eats, for God has accepted him. Who are you to judge the servant of another? To his own master he stands or falls; and he will stand, for the Lord is able to make him stand. One person regards one day above another, another regards every day alike Each person

must be fully convinced in his own mind. He who observes the day, observes it for the Lord, and he who eats, does so for the Lord, for he gives thanks to God; and he who eats not, for the Lord he does not eat, and gives thanks to God. For not one of us lives for himself, and not one dies for himself; for if we live, we live for the Lord, or if we die, we die for the Lord; therefore whether we live or die, we are the Lord's. For to this end Christ died and lived again, that He might be Lord both of the dead and of the living. But you, why do you judge your brother? Or you again, why do you regard your brother with contempt? For we will all stand before the judgment seat of God. For it is written, "AS I LIVE, SAYS THE LORD, EVERY KNEE SHALL BOW TO ME, AND EVERY TONGUE SHALL GIVE PRAISE TO GOD." So then each one of us will give an account of himself to God.

Romans 14:1–12

All things are lawful, but not all things are profitable All things are lawful, but not all things edify. Let no one seek his own good, but that of his neighbor. Eat anything that is sold in the meat market without asking questions for conscience' sake; FOR THE EARTH IS THE LORD'S, AND ALL IT CONTAINS.

If one of the unbelievers invites you and you want to go, eat anything that is set before you without asking questions for conscience' sake. But if anyone says to you, "This is meat sacrificed to idols," do not eat it, for the sake of the one who informed you, and for conscience' sake; I mean not your own conscience, but the other man's; for why is my freedom judged by another's conscience? If I partake with thankfulness, why am I slandered concerning that for which I give thanks? Whether, then, you eat or drink or whatever you do, do all to the glory of God. Give no offense either to Jews or to Greeks or to the church of God; just as I also please all men in all things, not seeking my own profit but the profit of the many, so that they may be saved.

1 Corinthians 10:23–33

God did not create any of us to convince others of their ignorance and error. Christian liberty frees us from having to argue, criticize, look down upon others, or worry about things we don't know and can't control. We need to carefully distinguish between our personal convictions and biblical directives. We can live for Him without being offensive to others and thereby minister to them and honor God.

Take notice that I am talking about ministering to other Christians. It is a completely different topic to talk about non-Christians. The gospel, while preached to them in love and truth, may very well be offensive, and that should not deter me from preaching it anyway.

The last thing that needs to be said is that liberty in Christ is something that needs to be looked at very carefully in one's own life and respected. Liberty can be like reckless words. If expressed improperly, it can do more harm than good to others and us. It is not a liberty to act self-righteously. A lot of people tromp through life completely oblivious to the destruction that their misguided piety produces. Liberty is not about taking a stand for Christ at the expense of other Christians' feelings or character. Remember, I am not talking about truth, which is always required when called upon; I am talking about liberty in Christ. It is not a license to bash other people for the sake of making sure people know what we stand for, even if that something is Christ.

Christian liberty becomes more powerful as we become more mature in our faith. Those who experience liberty in Christ the most are those who are like the type I described in my introduction: the people who had patience with me, not those who gave me their pious chastising or got frustrated with me for not seeing things their way. I have very ignorantly hurt many people in my life by doing just that.

If the Holy Spirit has not convinced someone of something that you consider to be a concrete truth, your wagging finger is not going to be the voice of God that will change his or her mind. Christian liberty is a grace for us to apply love to minister to others. If God intends for them to change, it will be His Spirit that convinces them, not our righteous indignation.

Total Depravity

In order for us to come full circle and appreciate liberty, I think we should spend a moment talking about total depravity. Some people have a hard time with the notion of total depravity. Total depravity basically means that there is nothing good in man apart from the righteousness of Christ. They want to believe that it is possible for some human who does not know Christ (and therefore God) to be able to produce "good." They do not accept the statement that without Christ, there is only sin and the promise of death. God may produce good from man's wickedness, but man cannot.

I look at people I know in my life, and I see some who have rejected Christ, and yet I see what appears to be so much kindness and goodness in their lives. I must go back to Scripture and let Scripture explain my experience and not let my experience explain Scripture.

The Bible states very clearly that the only good God accepts is the righteousness of Christ. What we call good in this life is still not the perfect reflection of God's glory that He intended. Many people have the mistaken idea that once they experience salvation, they are now able to do good and please God. The truth is, however, that it is not them that God is pleased with, but Christ. It is the righteousness of Christ that is placed on them that God sees and accepts. I am still the same person I was before salvation, but now God sees me *in Christ*!

It is important to note that Christians and non-Christians can behave in the same manner. Both can have successful marriages, be generous, patient, and kind, and even go to church. I have very close friends in this life who do not know Christ, and they are very nice people who do good things, but they are not covered in the righteousness of Christ. That is the only difference between them and me, not some ability I now possess that allows me to do good.

I must go back to Scripture and let Scripture explain my experience and not let my experience explain Scripture.

Again, the only thing that I can do "better" than them is reflect the Image of God purposefully by willfully giving Him glory. This includes repentance submitted to God's authority.

Maybe if more of us Christians stopped acting like we are better people than non-Christians, non-Christians would be able to hear that it is only the righteousness of Christ that is counted as good. Maybe then they would not get caught up in the futile question, "How can a good God allow a good person to go to hell?" The proper question to ask is, "How can God allow any of these other people to have eternal life?" Christians are unable to point to themselves just the same as non-Christians are unable to point to themselves. A worldview change leads to a proper perspective. The emphasis is properly placed on Christ. Liberty, like salvation, is a gift from God alone, not a benefit of man's efforts.

Putting It Together

In the real world, perfect scenarios are not always possible. Sin has infected every part of life so deeply that even good situations like fellowship or seemingly simple statements can cause division. God's provision of liberty is an empowerment to glorify Him through living for Him in the midst of those less than ideal situations. That doesn't mean that whatever we do with good intentions will please Him. We still need to look into God's Word and discern His good and perfect will so that when we do make choices, those choices align with His will and not just ours.

What is God's will? His Glory through peace, unity, and love. How do I live that right now? By using the liberty I have in Christ to maintain peace, unity, and love with my brother and sister in order that God will be glorified. It is easier said than done, but when I focus on the righteousness of Christ and not my "good," the Image is reflected.

Conscience and the Holy Spirit

What does conscience mean to you? Is it a quasi-spiritual part of your soul that communes with the Holy Spirit to guide you into all truth? Is it a state of being? Is it something that allows you to discern God's will for life? This is something that everyone needs to think seriously about as they strive to bear the Image by living out the will of God without abusing the liberty they have in Christ.

The conscience and the Holy Spirit are not the same things. Remember that commandment that says not to use the Lord's name in vain? I think this commandment is probably broken here more than in any other place in life; people misrepresent their own conscience as the authority or influence of the Holy Spirit. For example, people will say not to utter "Oh my God" or other uses of His name that are less than holy. The commandment to not take the Lord's name in vain does not mean to avoid using the Lord's name as an explicative. That is completely out of context, and the word translated as "vain" has nothing to do with the meaning of "cursing."

People in ancient Israel were not going around saying

"Yahweh!" when they hit their thumb with a hammer. They didn't say "Oh my El Shaddai!" when they were shocked with fright. What they were in danger of doing was using His name to give authority to something that they wanted to have unchallenged. The surrounding nations would say things like, "Thus sayeth Baal..." Obviously Baal never said anything; he was fictitious. Men were just trying to push their own agendas. God said, "Don't even try doing that with Me! I am a holy God, and you will not use My name in a manner to try and manipulate Me or others!"

So, when people today say things like, "God says in the Bible..." they need to make sure they study what they are quoting. It's ironic that people who quote this commandment and apply it to cursing are actually breaking the commandment. They may mean well, but meaning well does not excuse poor stewardship of the spoken Scripture.

People who mean well may do so according to their own understanding or their own worldview that is not necessarily founded on the worldview that Scripture presents. Speaking for God out of an understanding of Scripture that has no solid exegesis, but is based on personal life experience, can be a deadly practice. Personal experience is not a substitute for studying the Word of God.

Let me remind you that the point of this book is to help you develop a sense of joy as you experience the profound responsibility and freedom of bearing God's Image and living out His will for life in general. All of this "talking" does nothing if it does not lead you to a point where you can experience those truths. So what does this chapter have to do with bearing the Image of

God and living out His will? First, let's look at what Scripture tells us about our conscience.

> For this finds favor, if for the sake of conscience toward God a person bears up under sorrows when suffering unjustly.
>
> 1 Peter 2:19

> But sanctify Christ as Lord in your hearts, always being ready to make a defense to everyone who asks you to give an account for the hope that is in you, yet with gentleness and reverence; and keep a good conscience so that in the thing in which you are slandered, those who revile your good behavior in Christ will be put to shame.
>
> 1 Peter 3:15–16

> How much more will the blood of Christ, who through the eternal Spirit offered Himself without blemish to God, cleanse your conscience from dead works to serve the living God?
>
> Hebrews 9:14

> Therefore, brethren, since we have confidence to enter the holy place by the blood of Jesus, by a new and living way which He inaugurated for us through the veil, that is, His flesh, and since we have a great priest over the house of God, let us draw near with a sincere heart in full assurance of faith, having our hearts sprinkled

clean from an evil conscience and our bodies washed with pure water.

Hebrews 10:19–22

While our responsibility to glorify God through the living of our life is paramount to the purpose of being human, we need to be careful that we never forget that bearing the image does not equate with being his mouthpiece. The Scripture is his mouthpiece.

We are commanded to keep it clear in 1 Peter 2:19, 3:15–16, and again in Hebrews 9:14, 10:19–22, we are told in context that our conscience can be cleansed. This means we do have some responsibility of the development of our conscience. We can submit it to Christ or develop it on our own. But even after we submit it to Christ, we are still responsible for developing it in Christ.

Scripture tells us that it is our work to develop our conscience through discipline under the instruction of God's Word.

> Concerning him we have much to say, and it is hard to explain, since you have become dull of hearing. For though by this time you ought to be teachers, you have need again for someone to teach you the elementary principles of the oracles of God, and you have come to need milk and not solid food. For everyone who partakes only of milk is not accustomed to the word of righteousness, for he is an infant. But

A.M. Lamouria

solid food is for the mature, who because of practice have their senses trained to discern good and evil.

Hebrews 5:11–14

Now for this very reason also, applying all diligence, in your faith supply moral excellence, and in your moral excellence, knowledge, and in your knowledge, self-control, and in your self-control, perseverance, and in your perseverance, godliness, and in your godliness, brotherly kindness, and in your brotherly kindness, love. For if these qualities are yours and are increasing, they render you neither useless nor unfruitful in the true knowledge of our Lord Jesus Christ. For he who lacks these qualities is blind or short-sighted, having forgotten his purification from his former sins.

2 Peter 1:5–9

My son, let them not vanish from your sight;
Keep sound wisdom and discretion,
So they will be life to your soul
And adornment to your neck.
Then you will walk in your way securely
And your foot will not stumble.
When you lie down, you will not be afraid;
When you lie down, your sleep will be sweet.

Proverbs 3:21–24

Therefore, our conscience can be trained according to a biblical worldview or a secular worldview. Scripture further warns us that if we choose the latter, our conscience will become defiled and thus seared and hardened (proud and obstinate).

> But the Spirit explicitly says that in later times some will fall away from the faith, paying attention to deceitful spirits and doctrines of demons, by means of the hypocrisy of liars seared in their own conscience as with a branding iron.
>
> 1 Timothy 4:1–2

> To the pure, all things are pure; but to those who are defiled and unbelieving, nothing is pure, but both their mind and their conscience are defiled.
>
> Titus 1:15

> But encourage one another day after day, as long as it is still called "Today," so that none of you will be hardened by the deceitfulness of sin.
>
> Hebrews 3:13

> So this I say, and affirm together with the Lord, that you walk no longer just as the Gentiles also walk, in the futility of their mind, being darkened in their understanding, excluded from the life of God because of the ignorance that is in them, because of the hardness of their heart; and they, having become callous, have given themselves over to sensuality for the practice of every kind of impurity with greediness.
>
> Ephesians 4:17–19

——————————— A.M. Lamouria

This command I entrust to you, Timothy, my son, in accordance with the prophecies previously made concerning you, that by them you fight the good fight, keeping faith and a good conscience, which some have rejected and suffered shipwreck in regard to their faith. Among these are Hymenaeus and Alexander, whom I have handed over to Satan, so that they will be taught not to blaspheme.

1 Timothy 1:18–20

Paul warns Timothy in 1 Timothy 1:18–20 not to become like others who have blasphemed God because their conscience was not strong enough to guard the faith they received. In verse 19, he distinguishes between the faith (a gift of God, not of ourselves, Ephesians 2:8) and a strong conscience (a product of our own learning, 1 Corinthians 8). We are his representatives, and we are commanded to speak the truth in love, but the truth we are commanded to speak is already written down and revealed in full.

Eugene Peterson gives a great paraphrase of Paul s instruction to his young protégé in 2 Timothy:

Retain the standard of sound words which you have heard from me, in the faith and love which are in Christ Jesus. Guard, through the Holy Spirit who dwells in us, the treasure which has been entrusted to you.

2 Timothy 1:13–14

Paul is pretty emphatic to Timothy that the message he is entrusted with is a product of God's grace, not of any man's eloquence or education. This is where we need to be careful with the audacity with which we preach. We need to spend a good amount of time studying the Word and will of God before we speak on His behalf. It helps to have a community of fellow students around you that can challenge your thoughts, hold you accountable to the context, and share with you insights you may have not been open to. As students consider seminary, I like to remind them of this point.

So what's the point of all this?

The Burden of Learning

Personal experience is not a substitute for studying the Word of God.

The word conscience means "with knowledge." The purpose of conscience is not to guide to a proper understanding of God's will, nor is this to be attributed to the work of the Holy Spirit within us. Conscience is only the product of our knowledge. It can only guide us according to what we have learned. This is why our learning needs to be founded in the biblical worldview and built up by studying the wisdom in Scripture.

Some people have stronger consciences than others because they have learned more in regard to God's revealed moral will. A strong conviction, however, is not a sign of a strong conscience. Some people have learned faulty knowledge, and thus their conscience misguides them, even though their conviction to their conscience is great. Paul talks about this exact thing in 1 Corinthians.

However not all men have this knowledge; but some, being accustomed to the idol until now, eat food as if it were sacrificed to an idol; and their conscience being weak is defiled.

1 Corinthians 8:7

The point is that your conscience is not the voice of God. If you know someone that thinks his or her conscience is a standard by which all things must be measured and that their conscience cannot change, then I would encourage you to gently and respectfully warn them against self-righteousness and arrogance. We can always learn more and grow.

Our conscience should lead us to humility and trembling before an almighty God any time we choose to speak on His behalf. He has given ample warning in his Word about using His name in vain or teaching things in His name that have been so twisted that they no longer reflect His revealed truth. Check out a sample of the verses that deal with this topic:

You shall not swear falsely by My name, so as to profane the name of your God; I am the Lord.

Leviticus 19:12

But the prophet who speaks a word presumptuously in My name which I have not commanded him to speak, or which he speaks in the name of other gods, that prophet shall die.

You may say in your heart, 'How will we know the word which the Lord has not spoken?'

When a prophet speaks in the name of the Lord, if the thing does not come about or come true, that is the thing which the Lord has not spoken The prophet has spoken it presumptuously; you shall not be afraid of him.

Deuteronomy 18:20–22

"… because they have acted foolishly in Israel, and have committed adultery with their neighbors' wives and have spoken words in My name falsely, which I did not command them; and I am He who knows and am a witness," declares the Lord.

Jeremiah 29:23

BUT IN VAIN DO THEY WORSHIP ME, TEACHING AS DOCTRINES THE PRECEPTS OF MEN.

Matthew 15:9

The more we learn about God's Word and God's will, the more our conscience is strengthened to be more susceptible to the Spirit's leading and calling. As our conscience grows in this way, our recognition of the Spirit's direction becomes more acute. The key thing to remember here is that the conscience is under man's control. God does not take over our conscience when we are redeemed. He allows us to grow and demands that we continue to learn His will according to His word so that our conscience does not become idle and useless (2 Peter 1).

Listening to the Spirit

The more we learn about God's Word and God's will, the more our conscience is strengthened to be more susceptible to the Spirit's leading and calling. Many people have a problem accepting this statement because they want to believe that God leads them into all truth regardless of their attention to His leading or their effort in pursuing it. The problem with this thinking clearly arises when we see two different God-fearing Christians disagreeing over what is professed by both parties as "clearly stated biblical truth." Faith is not magic. It does not automatically make us think and perceive all things the way God wants us to.

In John 16:13, Jesus tells his disciples, "When the Spirit of truth comes, He will guide you into all truth." Many people quote that passage today as if it is some kind of testimony as to how a solitary Christian can come to understand all the truth of Scripture simply by themselves. This is bad Bible study and probably one of the most destructive misunderstandings in the Church today. Not everyone is equipped to handle the Word of God rightly. They could be if they pursued the discipline of study correctly, but not everyone does.

First of all, let's take a look at the context of this verse. Jesus is nearing the end of a very private discussion with His disciples. The discussion begins in chapter 13 in the upper room as Jesus is preparing them for His departure with final instructions and exhortations. In chapter 13, our Lord says:

> From now on I am telling you before it comes
> to pass, so that when it does occur, you may
> believe that I am He. Truly, truly, I say to you,

he who receives whomever I send receives Me; and he who receives Me receives Him who sent Me.

John 13:19–20

This is a very powerful indicator of what Jesus is talking about in John 16:13 above. Jesus is talking to his disciples, not everyone. He is giving them something that they need to know in order to be comforted in what is about to happen to them specifically.

Since Jesus is talking only to His disciples and His words are meant to comfort them, what is it that He is talking about in 16:13? Well, remember that up until the miracle of Christ's appearance to the disciples in an upper room after His resurrection, none of the disciples had a spiritual mind. Many people like to argue this point, but Scripture clearly tells us that the unspiritual mind cannot understand spiritual truths, and the Bible clearly says that none of the disciples understood what Jesus was telling them most of the time. They believed He was the Messiah, the Son of the living God (Matthew 16:16), but they didn't understand what exactly that meant, the full ramifications of that truth. Remember, to them, "messiah" meant "anointed one." David was a messiah to them as well. So was Moses. Many people in their history were.

We know they didn't fully understand because immediately after Jesus admonishes Peter as the rock of the Church's foundation in Matthew 16:18, He rebukes Peter seven verses later as an "offense" and calls him "Satan" because he doesn't have the things of God in mind, but the things of man. Peter wanted Jesus to be the messiah he had in his mind, not the predicted messiah of the

Torah he was taught as a child. That was a very important and very big difference.

The disciples didn't have a spiritual mind until the Holy Spirit came into them at Christ's bidding after his resurrection (Luke 24:45, John 20:22). The first sermon isn't delivered by any of them until the day of Pentecost when Peter gave his first sermon to the collective who had also received the Holy Spirit and could understand (Acts 2). In Mark 6, we see Jesus send out the disciples two by two, but at that time, it was only to preach repentance. Physical healing was an added bonus, but they didn't understand anything more of the salvation gospel yet. Only two and three chapters later, we see the rebuking of Peter and the ignorance of the others regarding the central purpose of Jesus's ministry.

So now, let us return to John 16:13. Jesus wasn't telling His disciples that the Holy Spirit would guide each of them into a full understanding of everything spiritual. Again, Jesus said, "When the Spirit of truth comes, He will guide you into all truth." What is the significance of this statement?

First, Jesus is telling the disciples that they are going to be led into the truth of something that they don't fully understand at this point. He goes on to tell them in the following two verses that what they will learn has something to do with what belongs to the Father and the Son together.

> He will glorify Me, for He will take of Mine and will disclose it to you. All things that the Father has are Mine; therefore I said that He takes of Mine and will disclose it to you.
>
> John 16:14–15

So the question is: What will the disciples need to know very shortly that they don't fully understand right at this point and that also has to do with something that the Father and the Son share? The answer is the shared deity and glory of God. Jesus was preparing His disciples for the impending crisis of faith they would face in several hours. They would hide in fear in an upper room after the death of Christ. They would go back to fishing from not knowing what else to do. But nonetheless, Christ would demand of them to bring the Gospel message of His glory and grace to the rest of the world. They had been prepared, but they wouldn't "get it" in all its fullness until the day of Pentecost when Peter recognized the prophecy of Joel fulfilled.

John 16:13 is specifically for the eleven disciples who would not betray Him. The Holy Spirit would guide them into all truth that built off three years of Jesus's teaching so that they could give us the message that Jesus is God, and God alone did what needed to be done. John 16:13 is intended to give the reader confidence in the message of the twelve disciples (Matthias was included by the time of Pentecost). It is not a guarantee that if we simply read the Bible as a Christian, we will understand what we read.

That is why study and accountability are such a critical piece of Paul's message throughout the New Testament. It is very fearful (holy fear) work to study, discern, and preach the Word of God rightly. If more Christians respected this, there would be far fewer false teachers masquerading as pastors of "postmodern churches" and "movements" today. False teaching would simply be more easily recognized. This is something you need to be aware of. You need to look for a church that encourages solid biblical teaching any time you make a life transition that leads you to a new place. You cannot listen to the Spirit if you are not already paying attention to what is revealed in His Word.

Listening to the Spirit does not mean following our gut feeling. Feelings are fickle. It means pursuing His will for living by responding to His prompting of truths that are already stored away in us through study and observation. In other words, if you come to a moral crossroads and need to make an informed decision on say, having sex outside of marriage, listening to the Spirit involves responding to the truths that Scripture teaches about such an action. What feels like the most powerful pull or the right decision at the moment has nothing to do with it.

Make no mistake, the Spirit is living inside of us and will prompt us outside of our intellect, but listening to His Spirit means applying what the Spirit is prompting us to do based off of what we already know to be true from His Word, not what feels logical in our individual circumstances. Isn't it interesting that Jesus very often silenced the proud and overzealous by referring them back to what they already knew so well from Scripture? Studying the Word is the only way to strengthen our attentiveness to what the Spirit is saying, because He won't say something not already revealed there.

Putting It Together

Our conscience is our responsibility. It is only as effective as the bank account from which we make withdrawals. Each time we use discernment, make a decision, try to communicate our values, judge between right and wrong, or use our gifts to minister to others or worship, we are drawing from our bank account of biblical under-standing. The only way to invest in this bank account and make it more secure is to study God's Word under competent instruction. The more we learn, the stronger our conscience becomes and thus the more susceptible we are to the Spirit's guidance.

Again, your conscience is your responsibility. How are you developing yours as an Image Bearer?

The Image-Bearing Church: Our Place and Responsibility in the Body

You may have noticed that I have included a section at the end of every chapter titled "Putting It Together." If you have moved through the text with me in the order that I have presented the chapters, you will have noticed that each "Putting It Together" section combines all the main thoughts of every section up to that point. It's a building block approach to forming a worldview that is not only theologically acceptable but applicable to God-glorifying, practical action.

Well, here is the last piece to that building block approach in this book. We began by discussing what a worldview is and where God intended for us to get ours. Then we looked at how God intends us to apply that worldview to the rest of Scripture for learning and spiritual growth. Having built that solid foundation of knowing what we believe and why, we looked at how it changes our pursuit of a God-glorifying life from trying to figure out some mysterious predestined vocation to a daily expression of gratitude and holiness through the God-honoring stewardship of our gifts, abilities, and responsibilities. From there, we looked at how living a life as such brings us true freedom and allows us to exercise the freedom we have in Christ. The fifth building block was to understand how our conscience acts as it governs this life we live. Now we have come to the final building block.

The Christian Life

The "Christian life." What does that term make you think of? Hopefully it brings to mind the purpose for human existence as an Image Bearer, something about enjoying and glorifying God forever. Maybe now it makes you consider the stewardship of gifts and responsibilities that have been given to you in your life. Does it make you think about fellowship, evangelism, kindness, patience, or devotions? Does it make you think about service to others? Again, the question would probably elicit as many answers as the number of people asked. There would certainly be some consistencies, but I wonder what those consistencies would be if I asked people whose only perspective would be formed from watching your life?

My intent would be to find out if people knew anything about the body of Christ from watching your life. Do others get the idea that the Christian life is about the individual, or do they understand that the Christian life is about being a part of the body of Christ? Is your motto "Me and my Bible and my God"? Or is it more along the lines of, "Me and the Body living in the Word together for the Glory of God"?

"What's the point?" you ask.

The point is that Christ gave His life for His church,
His "bride," His "body." Those terms are never given to
the individual—they are given to the corporate collection of the redeemed. Many people like to philosophize
and say that Christ would have died for you even if you
were the only one ever created. True, He may have. But
the fact remains that Scripture was not created to be a
what-if scenario. You aren't the only one. The world is
full of the redeemed.

> For even as the body is one and yet has many
> members, and all the members of the body,
> though they are many, are one body, so also
> is Christ. For by one Spirit we were all bap-
> tized into one body, whether Jews or Greeks,
> whether slaves or free, and we were all made
> to drink of one Spirit. For the body is not one
> member, but many. If the foot says, "Because I
> am not a hand, I am not a part of the body," it
> is not for this reason any the less a part of the
> body. And if the ear says, "Because I am not an
> eye, I am not a part of the body," it is not for
> this reason any the less a part of the body. If
> the whole body were an eye, where would the
> hearing be? If the whole were hearing, where
> would the sense of smell be? But now God has
> placed the members, each one of them, in the
> body, just as He desired. If they were all one

member, where would the body be? But now there are many members, but one body.

And the eye cannot say to the hand, "I have no need of you"; or again the head to the feet, "I have no need of you." On the contrary, it is much truer that the members of the body which seem to be weaker are necessary; and those members of the body which we deem less honorable, on these we bestow more abundant honor, and our less presentable members become much more presentable, whereas our more presentable members have no need of it. But God has so composed the body, giving more abundant honor to that member which lacked, so that there may be no division in the body, but that the members may have the same care for one another. And if one member suffers, all the members suffer with it; if one member is honored, all the members rejoice with it. Now you are Christ's body, and individually members of it.

1 Corinthians 12:12–27

Brethren, even if anyone is caught in any trespass, you who are spiritual, restore such a one in a spirit of gentleness; each one looking to yourself, so that you too will not be tempted. Bear one another's burdens, and thereby fulfill the law of Christ. For if anyone thinks he is something when he is nothing, he deceives himself.

Galatians 6:1–3

A.M. Lamouria

AND HE CAME AND PREACHED PEACE TO YOU WHO WERE FAR AWAY, AND PEACE TO THOSE WHO WERE NEAR; for through Him we both have our access in one Spirit to the Father. So then you are no longer strangers and aliens, but you are fellow citizens with the saints, and are of God's household, having been built on the foundation of the apostles and prophets, Christ Jesus Himself being the corner stone, in whom the whole building, being fitted together, is growing into a holy temple in the Lord, in whom you also are being built together into a dwelling of God in the Spirit.

Ephesians 2:17–22

Christ's intention was that the redeemed live out their lives in community in order to fulfill His purposes and engage every part of life together.

The Great Image

Now that we have worked through all these steps to arrive here, I want to go full circle and talk about what it means to be an Image Bearer again. God has an Image Bearer in you, but much more significantly, He has an Image Bearer in the Church.

Think of all the religions of the world that employ some type of idol image upon which to focus their worship. Every religion of Abraham's day created some image formed by man's hands to represent its deity. When God finally gave His Ten Commandments to Moses, He told Moses that His people would have no manmade images. He had already created an image that represented Him, though not for the purpose of receiving worship; these images would actually do the worshiping!

How awesome is that? God's Image Bearers would not be made for others to worship, but for the purpose of glorifying Him through living out His will. Living images! While the rest of the world lives to serve lifeless idols, God is worshiped by a great, living Image. While the rest of the world needs to fashion representatives of their god's power, God has fashioned His own representatives, which will prove His power through their weaknesses!

The heart of this great privilege, however, is found in the Church. In Ephesians, Paul teaches this:

> And He put all things in subjection under His feet, and gave Him as head over all things to the church, which is His body, the fullness of Him who fills all in all.
>
> Ephesians 1:22–23

Read Ephesians 1. Paul is exhorting the Christians in Ephesus about all that God has done for them. He uses words like *blessed, chosen, predestined, adopted, and lavished upon* to describe the blessings they had received from God as new creations. However, the descriptive blessings are given to the Church. Christ is the head of His Body. His Body is the Church. The fullness of the Image of Christ in the world today is the expression of His likeness through the life of the Church!

I want to challenge you. Are you living in the Great Image? This isn't a biblical term, but it is a poignant, visual picture for believers today. You have been baptized by His Spirit into a family that lives for and represents His glory on this earth.

Many people today think that their relationship with Christ is only about them and their personal experiences. That couldn't be more false. Salvation through grace alone is a personal experience. The process of sanctification (life for every believer) is not. Sanctification is about life as a member of the Body. This is part of the nature of our God that confounds the world and eludes our understanding. Our God is community. He is three in one and one in three. The life He intends for us is community as well. You are in the Body if you are one of the redeemed.

Are You Obedient?

Are you being obedient to God through the stewardship of your purpose in the Body? If you are a hand, your purpose is to do "hand things" to edify the Body and glorify God. If you are a foot, your purpose is to do "foot things" to edify the Body and glorify God. If you are an eye, your purpose is to do "eye things" to edify the Body and glorify God. Are you doing your "things"? Are you doing your "things" to edify the Body or feel good about yourself? I would suggest that the Body of Christ in your area needs your "things" even if you don't know what they are. If you are seeking His will for your life by living what you already know is revealed in Scripture and you ask for wisdom, He will give it to you.

Somebody once told me that just showing up is 99 percent of success. Well, in Christianity, showing up properly is 99 percent of success. With God, we call that biblical faith. We show up, and He directs what happens from there. I'm not talking about salvation; I'm talking about what happens after salvation. We give our best at whatever we do for His glory and leave the results to Him.

Putting It Together

You were made to glorify God by exalting the name of Jesus Christ. You were made to do this as an Image Bearer. You are a living Image, but you are not alone. The Church is the Body of Christ, and as such it is also a living Image. As a redeemed citizen of the new creation, you are in that Body, whether or not you attend church. Being involved in that Body is a matter of obedience, because that is where the fullness of Christ is lived out. God is not made most apparent in this world through the pious humility or great accomplishments of any one man. He is made most apparent through the weaknesses of a billion believers committed to living together for His glory.

Image Bearing and Stewardship: Life and Ministry

Have you ever asked yourself this question: "What is ministry?" Christians use the word *ministry* all the time. But the occult and the secular world use the word *ministry* all the time as well. What does that word mean?

Ministry is the stewardship of gifts and responsibilities that God has given to an individual or a body.

As we have looked at in this book, God baptizes every believer into the Body and gives every believer at least one gift to use to edify the Body in order to better glorify God by exalting the name of Christ. With that privilege comes awesome responsibility to steward those gifts and to work out the combined blessings of all those gifts to benefit the kingdom of God on Earth. This is ministry. It is through this stewardship that God works in His world today.

Think about that. The God of the universe who created all things and spoke existence into reality; the same God who spoke through prophets and miracles, signs, and in many different ways throughout time; the same God who came to earth as a man, actually became sin for you and me, and conquered death through resurrection; this same God lives in you and me through the Holy Spirit! God gave us this Spirit for life, and through this Spirit in us He works outward to the rest of Creation. Remember, the Body of Christ is His great living representative in Creation. It is this great Body that works out, with fear and trembling, the mysteries of God's Word and thereby manifests His glory and His works in the world. [4]

I believe in miracles, but I don't believe in miracles apart from the Body of Christ. I believe the link is prayer. Scripture is very clear that even prayer is a ministry. James 5:13–18 makes a dramatic point that God gives us the privilege of prayer to be involved in His work. Even where there are miracles that happen apart from the physical presence of Christians, I believe that God has risen the needs of that miracle in the hearts of His believers and the Body is praying that miracle into being. This is the incredible grace of God given to broken people living for His glory. He chooses to use us.

Why? Because we are His Image Bearers. It is not that we have earned it or have grown into such stature that we are capable of "helping" Him. It is because He chooses to display His incredible sovereignty and power through the weakness that is humanity in order that His involvement might be undeniable.

Wow!

What a privilege.

What an awesome God!

The "Lone Ranger" Minister

This brings us to a very interesting situation. It is a situation that you are able to see more and more today thanks to the aid of the Internet, the impersonal nature of mega-ministries, and the lack of accountability that "business" brings to disciple the immature within the Body.[5] It is the phenomenon of "solo ministers" who are not under the headship and authority of a local body of Christ, even if they attend a local body of Christ.

When I say solo ministers, I am talking about individuals who go out with an agenda to serve the Lord but do so without submitting themselves to the accountability and support of the body. Where I currently live, there is a gentleman who claims to be a minister and presents himself in evangelism tracts and in person as "Dr. So-and-so." The problem is that he is not a doctor and some of the stuff in his evangelism tracts is doctrinally unsound. His reasoning for this misrepresentation is that he has read enough books by doctors (of theology) that he is the equivalent. He passes out his tracts on cars in parking lots and even goes into other church buildings to hand his tracts to members of other church bodies. He's a lone-ranger minister using deceit and manipulation to gain a hearing.

I've seen similar things on college campuses where students who have a passionate idea about something spiritual produce a spiritual newsletter or start some kind of community worship without the spiritual oversight of someone holding them and their ideas accountable. Think about how destructive it would be if anybody who had an idea wrote whatever they wanted and passed it off as expert advice and sound doctrine. I've known several people like that.

We have already discussed the danger in living a Christian life apart from the Body; I submit to you that it is even more dangerous to attempt to serve the Lord apart from the Body.

Ministry is not meant to be done alone. It should be done under the headship of the Church whose headship is in Christ. Even as I am writing this book, I have submitted it to numerous individuals in my life and body who are competent to evaluate what I have written according to the standard of God's Word. They have given me feedback that holds me accountable to the truth that is the living Word and to the boundaries of my knowledge and gifts.

We do not live in the days of the prophets anymore, and God does not always audibly speak to us to give us personal affirmation or discipline. Today He gives us His word and His Body together with the Spirit (and always the three together) so that we may discern what is good and true and right. It is here that we find our affirmation and our correction when needed.

Remember that ministry is a responsibility to steward what we have been given. The proper stewardship of any ministry involves life within the body. There is an interesting story in the book of Acts about a man named Apollos. In the eighteenth chapter we learn about this great preacher who spoke with great passion and had great theological understanding. But in verses 24–28 we read that he had a problem of ignorance. He preached baptism, but he didn't know about Christ! Two godly believers had to take him aside and teach him what he was missing, and then he went on to win people over to Christ even more fervently than he had when he preached before. Had he submitted himself to a local body of believers prior to his public circuit of ministry, he would not have run into this almost disastrous pit-fall. God used the body of Christ to minister to Apollos, hold him accountable to his message, and then make him even more effective at his calling. The point for us is that we need to be good stewards of what we have been given. We need to know it and be open to accountability of it so that we may be the most effective Image Bearer possible.

Evangelism

I made the statement earlier that evangelism is a mandate for the Church, not the purpose of it. I hope that you understand what I mean by that at this point in the book, but if not, let me elaborate.

Christ did not say about the church, "You came to seek and save the lost." He said of Himself in Luke 19:10, "I came to seek and save that which was lost." Christ came to redeem the Image of God in His creation (literally, "that [one] thing which was lost"). He accomplished that. It is finished. He did tell the disciples as He was leaving, however, that as they went into all the world, they were to teach all that He had commanded. The gospel message is only the tip of the spear of what He taught. The rest of the story is intended for godly instruction to build up the saints, encourage, exhort, rebuke, and correct. That is discipling language for those who already know Him.

The purpose of the Church is to glorify God, not evangelize. Evangelism is necessary and a way of glorifying Him. But it is not the only way to glorify Him. The strongest message in the New Testament after the Synoptic Gospels is "to hold firmly to the faith once delivered," to "guard the truth," to "be firmly rooted and established," to be "transformed by the renewing of the mind." Paul tells Timothy to never cease "reading the Scriptures, exhorting one another, and teaching sound doctrine."

I have heard it said so many times that the Church is for the sick. No, it's not. It is for the redeemed. Christ said He came to heal the sick. Heal them, not just give them a place to belong. His purpose was to join them to the Body so they in turn would glorify God. The difference is that evangelism as a purpose is man-centered, while evangelism as a mandate supports the real purpose, which is God's glory.

In Mark 2:17, Jesus makes the infamously misquoted statement that it is the sick that need a doctor, not the healthy. He is responding to a question from scribes regarding His behavior, not declaring a purpose for an institution. He states that He came to call sinners, not the righteous. Jesus is the doctor, not the Church. He calls sinners to Himself and then grafts them into His Body once cleansed in his righteousness.

You can't be a part of the Body unless you are redeemed. The Church is supposed to reach out to the sick and make them aware of Christ's offer, which is made available to us, not pull in as many sick as we can and let them infect us. Guard, build up, and hold on to healthy, life-giving truth. Where? In the Church. Evangelism flows out from a healthy body. It happens outside. Evangelism is a mandate, not our purpose.

Discerning What You Hear

Paul teaches an invaluable lesson through his mentoring of Timothy in two letters to his young protégé. In 1 and 2 Timothy, Paul gives three standards by which hearers can confidently stand equipped to discern any teacher or teaching that they ever hear. It is simple but powerful; it's powerful because it is simple.

Paul tells Timothy that there are three keys to righteous teaching. Sound doctrine has at its core in an unmistakable manner:

1. The teachings of Christ, the prophets, and the apostles

2. An interest in unity and peace, and

3. The goal of clarity.

The Teachings of Christ, the Prophets, and the Apostles

Throughout the Old and New Testament, the followers of the one true living God are exhorted to heed the teachings that have been passed on to them from generation to generation and then from Christ or as given to the apostles. The letter to the Hebrews begins with this powerful reminder:

> God, after He spoke long ago to the fathers in the prophets in many portions and in many ways, in these last days has spoken to us in His Son, whom He appointed heir of all things, through whom also He made the world. And He is the radiance of His glory and the exact representation of His nature, and upholds all things by the word of His power When He had made purification of sins, He sat down at the right hand of the Majesty on high, having become as much better than the angels, as

He has inherited a more excellent name than they.

Hebrews 1:1–4

The exact expression of God's nature, the one who holds the universe together by will and word, has communicated to us what we need to know to live a life according to His will. To ignore this is to welcome death. The words of Scripture are the words of God.

Paul tells us over and over again in the two short letters to Timothy that the message once received must be handled properly and kept pure and undefiled from the useless bantering and false wisdom of men.

> As I urged you upon my departure for Macedonia, remain on at Ephesus so that you may instruct certain men not to teach strange doctrines, nor to pay attention to myths and endless genealogies, which give rise to mere speculation rather than furthering the administration of God which is by faith. But the goal of our instruction is love from a pure heart and a good conscience and a sincere faith. For some men, straying from these things, have turned aside to fruitless discussion, wanting to be teachers of the Law, even though they do not understand either what they are saying or the matters about which they make confident assertions.
>
> But we know that the Law is good, if one uses it lawfully, realizing the fact that law is not made for a righteous person, but for those who are lawless and rebellious, for the ungodly and sin-

ners, for the unholy and profane, for those who kill their fathers or mothers, for murderers and immoral men and homosexuals and kidnappers and liars and perjurers, and whatever else is contrary to sound teaching, according to the glorious gospel of the blessed God, with which I have been entrusted.

1 Timothy 1:3–11

This command I entrust to you, Timothy, my son, in accordance with the prophecies previously made concerning you, that by them you fight the good fight, keeping faith and a good conscience, which some have rejected and suffered shipwreck in regard to their faith.

1 Timothy 1:18–19

Pay close attention to yourself and to your teaching; persevere in these things, for as you do this you will ensure salvation both for yourself and for those who hear you.

1 Timothy 4:16

If anyone advocates a different doctrine and does not agree with sound words, those of our Lord Jesus Christ, and with the doctrine conforming to godliness, he is conceited and understands nothing.

1 Timothy 6:3–4

O Timothy, guard what has been entrusted to you, avoiding worldly and empty chatter and the opposing arguments of what is falsely called "knowledge."

1 Timothy 6:20

Jesus Christ said that men worship Him in vain, holding on to their own teachings while letting go of God's. They turn from God's truth in favor of their developed religious traditions (Mark 7:6–8).

Of all those verses mentioned before, the most important are probably 1 Timothy 6:3–5. Paul tells Timothy that anyone who teaches anything outside of Jesus's teachings and godly teachings (prophets and apostles who communicated wisdom given directly by God to them) is conceited and understands nothing!

The first sign of a godly teacher is that he or she spends his or her time teaching the Word of God with the Word of God doing the explaining. Many men and women today will preach a message disguised as the Word of God by reading the Scripture briefly and then expounding great spiritual truths therein using psychology and philosophical reasoning. Remember, the Bible must always explain life, not the other way around. The Bible speaks for itself.

A well-equipped teacher of the Word who knows how to rightly divide the Word will be a guide through the Scriptures, showing how the text examines and explains itself. My father told me when I went off to college, "If you want to find a church to attend, look for one where the people exit their cars with Bible in hand and the pastor leads them through inside." Follow a good leader, and a good leader will follow the Word.

An Interest in Unity and Peace

Over and over again in the verses I noted above and throughout the Bible, God instructs us to beware of useless arguments, those who cause needless strife, and quarrelsome teachers. The aim of God's revelation to mankind is to draw us closer unto Him and to each other.

In the final hours of Jesus's life, He prayed that we would be one as He and the Father were one and that we would be given to Him for eternity (John 17:10–26). It is amazing to think that our Creator loves us enough, despite our continued brokenness, to ask for us! Jesus doesn't desire to be with us—He desires us to be with Him. He doesn't want to be like us—He wants us to be like Him. He doesn't want us to simply be crowned with glory and honor—He crowns us as Image Bearers because He wants us to be involved in giving Him glory. Jesus wants us to be united with Him in this way.

But Jesus wants us to be united together as well. How much of the New Testament is written exhorting believers to be of one unified body and purpose? Why is love greater than faith and hope? Why does God use humans to reach other humans? Think about this: In Romans, Paul teaches us that people will not be saved apart from the use of other human beings.

> For "WHOEVER WILL CALL ON THE NAME OF THE LORD WILL BE SAVED." How then will they call on Him in whom they have not believed? How will they believe in Him whom they have not heard? And how will they hear without a preacher? How will they preach unless they are sent? Just as it is written,

"HOW BEAUTIFUL ARE THE FEET OF THOSE WHO BRING GOOD NEWS OF GOOD THINGS!"

Romans 10:13–15

God makes it so that we have to be involved in the work of kingdom building and soul saving. We don't do the saving, but we are His instruments of proclamation! Why? Because He wants us to be in the unity of community. Real community. Christ-centered community.

The story of Cornelius in Acts 10 and 11 is awesome because it demonstrates the incredible responsibility and privilege that God gives to us. The Bible teaches that Cornelius was a God-fearing man. An angel comes to him one day and tells him to send for Peter because he is not yet saved and needs to hear the gospel of Christ from Peter in order to be saved. The angel is right there! Why doesn't he tell him about Jesus and everything that has already happened for the salvation of mankind? God chooses to patiently use the time and distance considerations of having to send for Peter, Peter traveling, and everyone waiting until the end of Peter's presentation to save Cornelius and his whole household.

What if Cornelius had died? What if Peter had died? Aren't these the arguments we hear today when people argue that there must be more than one way to God, because of all the people in remote parts of the world who will never hear? This story, and the rest of Scripture, teaches us that God is sovereign. He has a plan, and He will save those whom He has chosen to save, and He will do it the way He designed it to happen. God doesn't make mistakes. He doesn't need a plan B. He knows what He is doing, and trusting that is called faith.

God uses us, and He wants us to be involved in each other's lives as Image Bearers. He cares about peace and unity. A Christ-centered, biblical teacher will be one whose message focuses on the Word of God and, in doing so, ultimately brings unity and peace to God's family.

The Goal of Clarity

Paul's words ring out over and over again in my mind:

> If anyone advocates a different doctrine and does not agree with sound words, those of our Lord Jesus Christ, and with the doctrine conforming to godliness, he is conceited and understands nothing; but he has a morbid interest in controversial questions and disputes about words, out of which arise envy, strife, abusive language, evil suspicions, and constant friction between men of depraved mind and deprived of the truth, who suppose that godliness is a means of gain.
>
> 1 Timothy 6:3–5

In today's world, we have so many teachers rising up and teaching "new insight" about God's truth and God's church. "We have never gotten it right," they say. They use clever words and very profound philosophical thought, but they deny the clarity and "objective knowability" of Christ and his Word. That means that they deny that there is one standard of truth. They claim that anyone can have their own interpretation and be okay with God as long as they intend well and really believe that they know Jesus and what Jesus meant for them personally. They say that no one can really know what the Bible means and teach it as though it were an understandable communication from God.

Let me tell you now, as I did in the introduction to this book, that I believe in the infallible nature of God's Word. I believe it can be known, it is meant to be known, and as we just discussed in our look at Cornelius, it can be communicated linguistically. God is a god of incredible clarity. There is nothing confusing about, "I am the way, the truth and the life. No one comes to the Father but through me" (John 14:6). If a teacher of God's Word stands up and leads you into a discussion that leads God's family to confusion as to what God taught and claims subjective truth, he or she is not a well-equipped teacher of God's Word. A good teacher teaches from the Word of God, promotes unity, and brings clarity to the Word of God by using the Word of God.

Obedience, Ministry, and Purpose

Ministry is accomplished when one lives out his or her purpose in life. This happens when we submit to the Word of God for our own lives and become obedient to His plan that is revealed within it. That's right. Let us not forget that God is always in control and that He is always working out His will and His plan. Obedience to God's Word leads to trusting God to accomplish what He said He would accomplish, which in turn leads to giving our lives to Him for His use and thus finding our specific purpose in the ministry that He has for us. There are three great distracters that make it difficult for us to trust God if we don't pay attention to our focus.

Faith in man versus faith in Christ: This means we have more faith in people's personalities and brokenness than we do in God's ability to change them or work through us to reach them despite their broken-ness. A typical symptom of this is frustration or non-compassion.

Faith in circumstances versus faith in Christ: This means that we place more faith in our circumstances of life (where we live, what family we are a part of, what opportunities we think we have, etc.) than we do in what Christ is able to do regardless of our situation. A typical symptom of this is apathy or depression.

Faith in sight versus faith in God's Living Word: This means we place more faith in what we see happening in the world around us, regardless of whether it impacts us or not, than we do in God's promises and covenant rela-tionship with us found in Scripture. A typical symptom of this is fear.

One thing we tend to do in our modern-day world is to confuse the obstinacy of man, the circumstances of life, or the appearance/presence of brokenness in the world with the ability of God. I talk to people all the time who live in the midst of difficult circumstances and difficult people. They rightly discern the need for Christ in the circumstances in order for change to occur. They pray for change and for patience, but then they turn around and make the most profound and self-defeat-ing mistake of all: They recognize the obstinacy of the people around them or the brokenness of life, and they doubt the ability of God to work change in life because of that distraction.

Remember this: The God of the universe lives within you. He does not submit to you or confine Himself to you, but He lives within you. He calls you to obedience. Your part is to live the way *you* are supposed to. He will work through you and His Body to do the rest. Give 100 percent to your responsibility and leave the results up to God.

Putting It Together

Obedience to the Word of God results in living out His will. This is ministry. To think that God has given anyone so significant and special a task that they do not need the Body or need its support is to deny the headship of Christ in the Church. Christ speaks about returning for His Bride, His Body, His Church. He does not say, "I will come back to pick up Jerry and Cynthia and Bob and Luke and Tony and…" God desires His Body to stand against the gates of hell. He does not desire that the lone ranger do it. And He has made it possible and fundamentally essential for it to be just that way.

Lessons Learned

It is one thing to look at life through the lens of Scripture and quite another to get out there and live it with that lens in focus. I hope that you can read this chapter in light of the previous chapters and then avoid or correct a few of the most significant problems that I came to understand in my own life through my formative years. You'll notice that all three of these issues are relational. There are a lot of issues that I could deal with, but I feel these three are the three most significant struggles for adolescents today starting out on their own journey. The reason is that as young adults, the most significant aspect of our lives is relationships, and we tend to struggle most in areas where relationships have been perverted by sin. I hope these speak to your heart.

Sex
(Why it hurts not to wait)

There are only two types of people when it comes to sex: those who have and those who haven't. That's it. Let's dispel this myth (or simply admit it is a lie) that there exists this gray area where "stuff" other than genital intercourse does not constitute sexually inappropriate behavior. We all know beyond the shadow of a doubt when we have crossed that God-honoring line (remember Romans 1).

Sex is not a difficult topic to approach; it is simply a difficult topic to talk about because the world and the Church alike have muddied the waters of truth. We have compromised the standard and truth of God with our own rationalized, selfish human nature to the degree where it is difficult for two God-fearing Christians to sit down with Bible in hand and agree on what God has to say about sex. Probably in no other area of life has so much deception so readily permeated the community of believers. Satan truly has mastered the battlefield of the mind when it comes to sex. God has one purpose and place for sex, and that is the marriage bed.

Sex is not a separate issue from the rest of the union of companionship in the creation narrative; it is an extension of it.

I grew up hearing about sex and the reasons to avoid it, but I didn't listen. I am regrettably one of the growing number of Christians today that gave in to little compromises bit by bit until I lost the battle in my own mind and was given over to my desires. I hurt several other people and myself because of my disobedience.

You've heard this before, though, so why is what I have to say different? What is the lesson learned? Please pay attention to this.

We need to begin with the beginning again. God made two people for each other. Do you understand the significance of that statement? *Made for each other. One made for one.* Sex is not a separate issue from the rest of the union of companionship in the Creation narrative; it is an extension of it. It is part of the union, plain and simple. God does not separate issues and talk about union and then turn around and talk about sex. They were never meant to be separated.

Sex outside of this intended union hurts you, the other person, and your spouse. Maybe you do not see the damage right away, but it will always eventually show up as pain. God calls this damage adultery. Adultery is a sin, and He constantly reminds His people in Scripture not to be adulterers in human relationships or in relationship with Him. It is the sin of being unfaithful to that one sacred union that was purposed.

I am not going to talk about the other people involved. While you are responsible for the consequences of your sin, I cannot address the behavior of others in response to that sin. What I can talk about is the pain that you experience after marriage because of premarital sex.

It's really as simple as this: you remember. Grace is an incredible gift. Forgiveness is a powerful force, but memory is a terrible thing when it comes to sin. There is nothing so vicious as your own mind reminding you of your failures. You know it by the name "shame." Someone once said that the one person in life that you most resent is yourself, because you are the one person that you can never get away from, and you are the one person that you know everything about!

You have probably experienced that situation in life where you see something or smell something or experience a situation that you once shared with some significant other. When that happens, you are flooded with memories of that person. You don't ask for it, you don't want to remember, you just do. Even if you try to replace those thoughts immediately, they have affected you somehow.

Here is where premarital sex becomes a consequence, even if it is not intercourse. You may have a wonderful marriage and a fulfilling marriage bed, and you believe there is no doubt or mistrust in your marriage, but when you begin to remember another person sexually that is not your spouse, you understand the pain of feeling unfaithful to your spouse.

God intended for a perfect union to be blessed with perfect joy in perfect intimacy. Please do not lie to yourself and say that grace will be sufficient for you to protect you from this. Grace is sufficient for salvation and security of the hope we have in Christ, but Paul himself testified that even he experienced emotional, mental, and physical pain in life due to his past despite being the foremost authority at understanding grace. Premarital sex robs you of the perfect joy that comes with that perfect union within marriage.

It is true that respect for others and respect for yourself is an issue. It is true that you will regret it after that person is no longer in your life. It is true that you can contract diseases or have children that you are not willing to support. These are all consequences that can happen, but the main travesty is the irreparable damage to God's purpose through disobedience. This is the sin of adultery. Do you bear the Image of God to your spouse or future spouse the way He intended for you to?

Respect for Parents
(The only commandment
with a promise clause?)

I titled this section as such because I think it represents one of the most destructive and misleading perspectives in Western adolescent culture. Many people are aware that the commandment to honor your mother and father is the only commandment with a promise. But many of us have taken that word promise at some point in our lives and replaced it with the word clause. That means we dismiss the brevity of the command and say to ourselves, "Oh, it's not that big a deal; life has changed." We reject the importance that God put on this commandment and excuse our behavior to cultural evolution.

Why do we do this?

Usually for one of two reasons: Either to excuse unrighteous behavior that is already present in our lives or to allow for unrighteous behavior we think we are finally entitled to express. The difference is past offenses you already committed or future offenses you plan to or want to commit. The rationalization sounds like this: "I will honor my parents if they respect me or treat me the way they are supposed to."

The difference between the promise and a clause is that the promise comes with a commandment that requires specified behavior of us regardless of whether or not we want the promised reward, and a clause requires specified behavior from us only if the other party does what they are supposed to. God's version of the commandment ends with a promise to reward obedience and discipline disobedience, not a clause. God is not saying,

"If you want long life, then do this; if not, don't worry about it."

How many Christians do you know that live out this commandment as if it was only a clause? I was one of them. I acted as if I only had to honor my parents if they respected my rights as a teenager, didn't embarrass or hurt me, didn't betray me, listened to me sincerely, admitted their wrongs, and stayed out of my business. If they did that, then I would honor them. If they didn't, then I was free to criticize them publicly, privately, and indiscreetly. That was not the image I was created to bear.

I heard Pastor James Macdonald say the following on the radio once:

> God commands all of His people everywhere to "honor your father and mother." From small children to middle-aged adults to older adults, we never outgrow the need to apply this biblical principle. It is for every race and every culture, regardless of your parents' success rating, whether they are living or not, and regardless of how you may feel about it. God says straight up, "Honor your mom and dad."
> Honoring your parents is an attitude of respect. It's the admission that says, "You are the person God sovereignly placed in my life." They may have failed you or hurt or disappointed you at times, but God commands all children to honor their parents for what they did right."
>
> Pastor James Macdonald
> "How to Honor Your Parents"
> (2007, Walk in the Word)

The word honor is a word that means "weight." To give honor to something is to give it "weightiness." In other words, to give it value. To honor is to value. Do our lives give value to our parents for who God has made them to be? This is where we need to start.

Honoring parents in today's culture is not as popular as proving one's own autonomy and earning the right to be respected as an adult. Today's culture encourages us to stand up for ourselves and demand respect. Everything from advertising to babies' clothes and toys express the opinion that we all need to be seen as or treated as little adults. That desire for a common ground among children and adults has invaded the home and, in many circumstances, the church. This, in turn, is eroding the fabric of honor and respect for parents. Self-image has taken a priority over the family image and the intentions of God's heart.

I believe if we trusted God's heart when reading this commandment, we would walk in holy, humble fear—and it would become a lot more important.

When we are young, we can't wait for adults to see us as equals and view us as mature. We forget that God is not only our Creator, but, if we are saved in Christ, He is our Father too. If we can't honor our earthly parents, how is it possible to honor Him? Dishonor of human parents is disobedience to a direct command of God given to all people for all time. We cannot live in blatant disobedience to God and call it honor. We cannot represent his image to those who know us best if we do not learn to love through honoring those we were given to.

Patience in Relationships
(The need for immediacy)

Paul paints a beautiful picture of love in the thirteenth chapter of his first letter to the Corinthians.

> Love is patient, love is kind and is not jealous; love does not brag and is not arrogant, does not act unbecomingly; it does not seek its own, is not provoked, does not take into account a wrong suffered, does not rejoice in unrighteousness, but rejoices with the truth; bears all things, believes all things, hopes all things, endures all things. Love never fails; but if there are gifts of prophecy, they will be done away; if there are tongues, they will cease; if there is knowledge, it will be done away.

> 1 Corinthians 13:4–8

One of the most beautiful experiences in life is being patient enough to be thankful for not doing something you would have regretted had you not been patient. In a world of e-mail, instant messaging, cell phones in ten-year-olds' pockets, iTunes, and every other form of instant communication, people have begun to fear the absence of immediate self-gratification. This is what immediacy is: immediate self-gratification.

It looks like this: Cindy calls to tell Dan that she wants to break up. Dan doesn't understand this. He thinks everything is going well. Cindy tells him that she just wants a little time on her own before they talk because she needs time to heal herself because this hurts. This further confuses Dan. If it hurts, why do it?

What does Dan do with his questions? He gets in his car, drives over to her dorm room, pounds on the door, and, face to face, demands an explanation. Dan wants answers right now. He doesn't care if Cindy needs time to think. He wants immediacy.

I have found that immediacy rarely works when anger or fear is involved. Fear and anger do not promote any of the virtues listed in 1 Corinthians 13. Immediacy in such cases promotes self-gratification. "I want answers now." "I want to be heard right now." And oftentimes, most poignantly, "I want to know right now that you are hearing me."

This problem isn't isolated to dating relationships; it's everywhere: employer/employee, teacher/student, friend/friend, parent/child, sibling/sibling, etc.

For the Christian, immediacy can be a thorn. Many of us will struggle with the need to have immediacy for the rest of our lives. We need to learn from the quiet few who have learned to utilize letters and journals to process their thoughts and articulate words so that they don't have to live with the regret of saying things that they regret in times of emotional turmoil.

This means that we need to be patient in relationships. Patient to let God work in other people's lives. Patient to let other people work things out in their human minds. Patient to take time in order to communicate in non-threatening ways.

High school and college can be two of the hardest places to develop patience in relationships. Most of the time, students are running a hundred miles an hour with over-packed schedules, and they have pretty open access to friends at all times. This type of fast-paced environment and immediate access fosters a belief that we deserve to have things resolved "right now." It's here that we need to develop the lifestyle of Christian discipleship by respecting the relational rights of the other six billion Image Bearers of this world and the inadequacy of our human brains to operate optimally under emotional stress.

The lesson here is to be patient and love unselfishly. Write. Process. Pray. James warns us that our speech can be more deadly than a raging forest fire and more powerful than a mighty wave. Heed the caution and return to the guidance in Philippians 4:8 before you enter into a difficult conversation. Be in a place where your mind is focused on things good, pure, true, lovely, and noble. Have the mind of Christ and use your speech as one who bears His Image.

Repentance
(In the end...)

In the end, no matter where you are or have been, there is grace. 2 Corinthians 5:21 states very clearly, "He made the one who did not know sin to be sin for us, so that we might become the righteousness of God in Him." Christ became sin so that we might become the righteousness of God. There are robes of righteousness, Christ's righteousness, waiting for us to don if we have been called to Christ. His work is finished. There is nothing more required for salvation. We are sons and daughters of the King, Creator, Savior, God. Hallelujah!

God's message began with something very powerful, though, and it needs to be brought up at this point. We were called from darkness to light for the glory of God. It is expected of us to put off the old and put on the new to become more like Christ. John the Baptist and Christ himself began their teachings with this message, "Repent!" In Mark 1:14–15 Jesus says, "The time has come, repent and believe the gospel."

No matter where you are or have been, if you are in Christ, you are a new creation. You have been freed from the slavery of sin, and you belong to Christ. If you are like me and you have already fallen, put it behind you. Press on toward the goal of your faith, which is to know Christ fully. You can't do this without repentance. You can't put off the old and put on the new until you turn from self and turn toward Christ-likeness. Paul told Timothy to be an example of purity in faith to the rest of the world who looks at him as "young." Let that ring in your ears. You can change your world if you repent and live for Christ. Then you live according to your worldview of being an Image Bearer for the purpose of glorifying God! Amen.

Epilogue

You have the most powerful tool known to man. It is called the Old and New Testament. From beginning to end, it is a story of God's revelation to mankind about His own glory, His purposes, and His will. The testament (Bible) is a testament of who God is. It is the living Word. And that living Word is alive inside of you. He has given you everything you need to complete His will for your life. Live that Word out for the rest of the world to see. But live it out with holy fear and reverence because you were not made for your own admiration or the world's. You were made to be a reflection of God's glory. This is awesome stuff. This is power for living. This is where transformation of life through renewing of the mind begins.

The Image of God is alive and active in the world today. You are an Image Bearer, and the Church of which you are part is the ultimate living Image. You know your purpose and where you belong; now live in it with confidence and power.

Endnotes

1. Jaroslav Pelikan, p. 10

2. Mark 12:28

3. Genesis 2:18–25; Romans 12:5, 9–11, 18:1; 1 Corinthians 12:31–14:1

4. 1 Corinthians 4:1

5. I am not saying all mega churches are bad. I am talking about the impersonal nature that is most easily recognized in mega churches that don't foster community. I have attended and been a member of some of the largest churches in America that fearfully foster God's design for unity.

Appendix:
Chapter Study Guide

Note to reader: These questions are intended for group study and discussion, but they will work for group or private study. Regardless, I encourage you to write your responses to these questions. The discipline of writing answers down may seem trivial, but it reinforces and empowers the author to more clearly articulate and own their thoughts. Practice this. It will make a big difference.

Introduction

Read Psalm 78. Is the author teaching new revelation or something already revealed?

What did the author have to pass on? According to the text, was it sufficient for glorifying God? What is the purpose of this teaching (verses 7–8)? What are the foundational spiritual truths that you have been taught in your life? Do they focus on you or God? Write down what your basic worldview is for why you exist and what your purpose in life is.

Chapter 1

Read 2 Timothy 3–4. Chapter 3, verses 6–7 offer a stark warning to those who would pursue their life passions, even always learning, but never coming to a knowledge of the truth. What are your life's passions? Have you surrendered those passions to the purpose of glorifying God? Make a list of your passions and then write how they can be used to glorify God.

Is there any area of your life in which you are still the main character? What will it take to make God the main character of that part of your life? What promises of God would it help to focus on in order to trust God with becoming the main character?

Chapter 2

What do you think about the statement, "God's main agenda is not the salvation of man, but His own glory"? Does this fit with your worldview?

Is the majority of your Bible study effort on secondary benefits of God's work or on the main agenda of God?

Take some time to glance at the section headings in the text of your Bible found in Paul's writings. What seems to be his primary concern most of the time?

Write down three goals for your Bible study efforts that can mature you in your Bible study. Share these with someone else.

Chapter 3

Read Ephesians.

If you are not sure how to seek God's will, what has been your pattern for seeking God's will in your life? What have you tried? Be honest. We cannot grow and mature unless we acknowledge our faults and seek to honor Him through biblical change.

What is God's general purpose for believers found in chapter 4? What are marks of a believer who is seeking out and living the will of God in his or her life?

How is Romans 12:1–2 fleshed out more fully in chapters 4–5 of this book?

Chapter 4

How do you know that you are free from slavery to sin?

Is Romans 7:14–25 a condemnation of believers or an affirmation of salvation? What in that passage can only be experienced by a redeemed individual?

What is liberty in Christ?

What are at least two liberties that freedom in Christ gives you? Where can you apply these in your own life immediately?

Chapter 5

How are we responsible for the development of our conscience?

How can the conscience be damaged? What provisions does God give for healing damaged consciences?

What does it mean that "the Spirit will guide you into all truth"? (John 16:13)

Is there an area or circumstance in your life that you need to repent of and make right with God and/or others because you have mishandled His holy Word? Try to accomplish this and share it with someone in your group.

Chapter 6

How is your image bearing responsibility the same as that of the Church's image bearing responsibility? How is it different?

What does the Bible say is the individuals' relationship to the Church? What is Christ's relationship to the Church?

How can you suggest church membership to a believing brother or sister who does not attend a church in a nonthreatening way? What will you tell them is the importance of it?

Chapter 7

What would you say is the biblical definition of a miracle? Do miracles still happen today? What is the difference if they do? What is the same if they do? What does Romans 10:13–15 offer as God's primary venue of working in the world today? Think of the story of Noah, the tower of Babylon, Abraham becoming a great nation, the exodus, the wall of Jericho, the defeat of Goliath, the fall of pagan nations, the discipline of Israel through exile, the birth of Christ, the spreading of the Gospel. What do they all have in common concerning the administration of God's will and miracles?

Are the lost part of the Church? Why is this even an issue?

Review

What is the biblical Worldview? Where does it come from?

What is the metanarrative? What are its four parts, and why is it important to know them?

Why is it important to have a worldview that starts in Genesis and not at the cross?

What is the most effective biblical way to know God's will? How do prayer, fasting, and fellowship help us find God's will?

What does it mean to be a "slave to Christ" and "free from the bondage of sin"?

How is the conscience different from the Holy Spirit? How do they relate?

Why is it important to belong to a church?

What is the purpose of the Church?

Bibliography

Guinness, Os. *Fit Bodies, Fat Minds: Why Evangelicals Don't Think and What to Do About It*. Baker Books, Grand Rapids, 1994.

Meadors, Gary T. Decision Making God's Way: A New Model for Knowing God's Will. Zondervan, Grand Rapids, 2003.

Pelikan, Jaroslav. Jesus Through the Centuries: His Place in the History of Culture. Yale University, 1985.

Wittmer, Michael E. *Heaven is a Place on Earth: Why Everything You Do Matters To God*. Zondervan, Grand Rapids, 2004.

e|LIVE

listen|imagine|view|experience

AUDIO BOOK DOWNLOAD INCLUDED WITH THIS BOOK!

In your hands you hold a complete digital entertainment package. Besides purchasing the paper version of this book, this book includes a free download of the audio version of this book. Simply use the code listed below when visiting our website. Once downloaded to your computer, you can listen to the book through your computer's speakers, burn it to an audio CD or save the file to your portable music device (such as Apple's popular iPod) and listen on the go!

How to get your free audio book digital download:

1. Visit www.tatepublishing.com and click on the e|LIVE logo on the home page.
2. Enter the following coupon code:
   4adb-3cbe-3e9f-e7d2-ee7f-3e23-c92f-e667
3. Download the audio book from your e|LIVE digital locker and begin enjoying your new digital entertainment package today!